INSPIRATION FOR A
MAN CAVE

INSPIRATION FOR A MAN CAVE

Fred Ash

ELM HILL

A Division of
HarperCollins Christian Publishing

www.elmhillbooks.com

Inspiration for a Man Cave

Published in Nashville, Tennessee, by Elm Hill, an imprint of Thomas Nelson. Elm Hill and Thomas Nelson are registered trademarks of HarperCollins Christian Publishing, Inc.

Elm Hill titles may be purchased in bulk for educational, business, fund-raising, or sales promotional use. For information, please e-mail SpecialMarkets@ ThomasNelson.com.

Library of Congress Cataloging-in-Publication Data

Library of Congress Control Number: 2019935213

ISBN 978-1-400325368 (Paperback)
ISBN 978-1-400325375 (Hardbound)
ISBN 978-1-400325382 (eBook)

FOREWORD

This book is for men.

When we get together at our favourite coffee shop, we like to talk about man stuff—carpentry, cars, fishing, sailing and sometimes gardening, among other things. We are not eager to brag about the fact that part of our weekend was spent in church. This book starts each day talking about those topics that men like and draws spiritual lessons from them.

Inspiration for a Man Cave shows that God speaks to us men in the ordinary, everyday activities of life. As Christians we are doubly blessed because we have the best of both worlds—the here and now and the world to come.

I started these devotional thoughts by reflecting on what I did each day. For example, I build a backyard shed from scratch and thought about how God builds our life and the life of the Church. I like to fish and I thought of how Jesus called Galilean fishermen to be "fishers of men." I planted a garden and thought of the parables of Jesus in which he talked about wheat and weeds.

Most of us are not theologians. That's OK. But we should at least be "spiritually minded." We can reflect on life and listen to what God is saying to us as we drive our cars, repair our houses, walk in the parks and engage with our families.

Inspiration for a Man Cave is meant to encourage you to listen for God in your day-to-day activities and then to begin a life of reflection, linking the word of God to your daily living.

Fred Ash

ACKNOWLEDGEMENTS

Writing even a small book like this requires the help of others. I want to say thank you to the many friends who encouraged me to assemble these thoughts into a format that other men could enjoy. Encouragement goes a long way, and without it this book could not have been written.

Special thanks to Ron McInnis in Sechelt, BC, whom I have never met but who supplied me with some of his pictures of vintage cars and trucks. His photos are amazing.

Thanks also to my friend Stan Walker of Barrie, Ont., for his advice relating to all things mechanical and for supplying some pictures from his classic car club.

Thank you to my wife Shirley for taking pictures of me during our many activities together on land and in water, and for sharing in so many common interests.

Thank you to my photographer son Jeremy Ash who supplied the cover photo for this book.

Thanks to all those men who allowed me to share in so many fishing and boating adventures with them over the years.

CONTENTS

PART 1

SHEDS

1. PLANS

A short while ago, I decided to build a shed in my backyard. As I reflect on this modest construction project, I realize that there are many lessons to learn from such an experience, not the least of which is learning how to use some of the power tools I collected over the years but was not able to use much because of constant employment-related transfers.

Lesson one: you have to have a plan. Before you buy lumber, purchase nails and accumulate shingles you have to have a plan. You can't just start building not knowing what you are going to build, or where. I have a very small backyard, so I had to downscale my dream shed to one about 7 ft by 6 ft. For such a small shed I did not want to purchase expensive plans, so I went on the Internet and downloaded free plans. Even then I had to change all the measurement to fit what I could build in the space available. Following the plans I made, I now have a shed that is perfect for my backyard.

The same is true in life. You have to have a plan if you are going to accomplish anything worthwhile. You can make your own plans or you can ask God, the Master Builder, to direct you. The choice is yours, but since you've never built a life before, I recommend getting the best advise available.

PROVERBS 3:6 (NKJV)

In all your ways acknowledge Him, and He shall direct your paths.

2. LAWS

I built my shed a few months after moving to a new city. Not knowing all the by-laws of the community, I thought it best to phone the city hall to find out what the local regulations were relating to building a shed in my backyard. Did I need a permit? What restrictions were in effect? What were the regulations I had to follow? I was told that if my shed was less than 11 ft high, I did not need a permit. The one restriction was that the shed had to be at least two feet from my fence. Within those guidelines, I was free to build to my heart's desire.

There are guidelines also within which we must build our lives. We all recognize the laws of nature and accept the fact that we must live within them. The law of gravity, for example, will not permit us to build a shed in thin air. God has also created moral and spiritual laws. We must recognize these and build our lives within them. There are general moral and spiritual laws like those contained in the Ten Commandments and the Sermon on the Mount. And there are specific guidelines that apply to each of us individually. As you build your life, contact the Divine Lawgiver and ask Him what the guidelines are for your life.

PSALM 119:1 (NRSV)

Happy are those…who walk in the law of the Lord.

3. Cost

Everything has a cost—including a back-yard garden shed. You can get quite fancy and build an elaborate structure using cedar and fancy mouldings and high-grade siding. Or you can build plain and simple using basic material. The choice is yours. But you will not likely build your shed for free. My shed is the basic type. In fact, all the framing

is used lumber from one of my previous projects, a deck on my trailer which I sold. So I saved money there. And when I bought shingles, I picked the packages that were broken open and got them at fifty percent off (the shingles were fine; it was just the plastic wrapping that was broken). I got the paint from the Habitat for Humanity ReStore at a bargain price. So my shed cost about $150 to build.

In life, no matter what we do we must always consider the cost. Jesus said, *"Suppose one of you wants to build a tower. Will he not first sit down and estimate the cost to see if he has enough money to complete it? For if he lays the foundation and is not able to finish it, everyone who sees it will ridicule him, saying, 'This fellow began to build and was not able to finish' (Luke 14:28–30, NIV).*

There is a cost to following Jesus. You will have to make sacrifices. You will have to surrender your will to God's will. You will have to deny yourself and take up your cross daily if you are going to truly be a Christ follower. But to choose the alternative is to lose your soul. Count the cost of the decision that will determine your eternal destiny.

MATTHEW 16:26

What good will it be for someone to gain the whole world, yet forfeit their soul?

4. SITE

 Every shed has to be built some-
where. You just can't build it
anywhere. As with all real estate, location is of prime importance. Since the
backyard of our property is small, I
chose one corner—the east corner—
on which to build. The west corner
was occupied by large, flat stones on
which I planned to put our garden swing. Besides, the stones were heavy and
would require a lot more work to move.

After measuring the ground and staking off the corners, I asked my wife
what she thought of this plan. She looked at the location, paused, scrutinized the
situation and made her decision. The shed, she said, will not work there. It will
have to go in the west corner because the angle of our irregular-shaped backyard
created more room there. In her opinion, the shed would look better there, and
work better as well.

So I pulled up my stakes, got out my pick and shovel and began the back-break-
ing, sweaty task of removing the heavy stones to build in the better location.

The same is true in life. Where we choose to build our lives is important.
Most of us will live in a number of different locations in our lifetime. Where we
live will influence how we live. A life lived in a city will be quite different from
one lived in the county. A life lived in the Far North will be different from one
lived in an African village. Ask God for advice and choose carefully.

GENESIS 12:1 (CEV)

The Lord said to Abram: Leave your country, your family, and your rela-
tives and go to the land that I will show you.

5. MATERIAL

My shed was not going to be a Taj Mahal. Nevertheless, I needed good, solid material that could stand the wind, rain and snow of the Canadian climate. Besides the pressure treated 4″ × 4″ skids, I selected pressure treated 2″ × 4″ lumber for the joist to support the floor. For the wall studs and the roof rafters, I used recycled 2″ × 4″ from a deck I dismantled when I sold my trailer last year. Then

I bought plywood sheeting, shingles and a good supply of nails and screws to put it all together. The shed would be built with a combination of new and used material.

It is important when building our lives that we also choose the right building material. We create our lives out of such things as relationships, beliefs, knowledge and experiences. The people we surround ourselves with make us stronger or weaker. The beliefs we embrace make us secure or insecure. The knowledge we acquire helps or blocks our progress. The experiences (including our careers and jobs) we engage in enable or hinder our potential.

As you build your life, choose your building material carefully, and remember, too, that some of the "old stuff" from previous generations is still useful today.

1 CORINTHIANS 3:12–13

If anyone builds on this foundation using gold, silver, costly stones, wood, hay or straw, their work will be shown for what it is, because the Day will bring it to light.

6. TEAMWORK

It is rarely a good idea to work alone on a building project. Even though for my small-shed project I might have managed most of the work myself, it was much more fun doing it as a family. In addition, the job was much easier when I had someone else to hold the end of a board. And things went faster when several people were working on different aspects of the project at one time. And then there was the safety aspect; if I had injured myself while working alone I could have been in big trouble. Besides all that there is the fact that everyone got to bask in the glory of the finished project. It didn't become a one-man job, but a team effort.

The same is true in Christian life. Service for Christ was never meant to be done alone. Even though sometimes you might not have any alternative, if the opportunity is there for you to invite others to join you in the work, do so. As with building, Christian service is easier, faster and more satisfying when you are able to share it with someone else. And if you become injured, in the sense of becoming discouraged or insulted, you have others to talk to about it. And when the work is completed, you can rejoice together because of God's grace to everyone.

MARK 6:7

Calling the Twelve to him, he began to send them out two by two and gave them authority...

7. FOUNDATION

Let me state the obvious— sheds have to be built from the bottom up. Therefore lay a good foundation. For my little garden shed this meant two solid pieces of pressure-treated 4 × 4 skids. The pressure-treated wood is more resistant to rot, fungi and insects than is untreated wood. Of course if you are a purist you would probably go for cedar, which does not require being chemically treated. However, that was beyond my budget. With my 4 × 4 treated skids as a foundation, I was ready to go.

Life also needs a good foundation. Jesus once told a story about two men, each of whom built a house. One built on sand, and one built on rock. When a storm came, bringing wind and water, the house built on the sand fell, but the one built on the rock stood firm (Matthew 7:24–28). Jesus went on to explain that a man who builds his life on Jesus' teachings is like a man who builds his house on solid rock. That life will stand in the storms of life. But the man who ignores Jesus' teachings is like one who builds his house on sand—that man's life is on shaky ground.

MATTHEW 7:24

Therefore everyone who hears these words of mine and puts them into practice is like a wise man who built his house on the rock.

8. Floor

I had already laid the foundation of my shed. Two solid pieces of pressure-treated 4 × 4s overlaid with sturdy 2 × 4s would hold up the shed nicely. The next job was to lay the floor. I went to the local building supply store and inspected the various 4 × 8 sheeting.

When the knowledgeable salesman asked what I wanted, I said, "Two sheets of half-inch plywood." I was thinking of cost and figured this would be cheaper.

"What is it for?" he asked, obviously sensing my inexperience.

"The floor of a shed I'm building," I replied.

"You'll need at least three-quarter inch plywood for a floor," he said, explaining that anything less than that would not hold any weight and would buckle.

I bowed to his superior knowledge of building material and purchased the ¾ inch plywood for the floor.

Once you have Jesus Christ as the foundation of your life, you must choose carefully what to build on that foundation. If you try to skimp and take the cheap and easy route, you may find that what you build is inadequate for the life situations that you will face later. Watching a ½-hour Christian TV show a week will not be adequate to build your faith. You need the ¾- to 1½-hour service at a real church on Sunday and then supplement this with a ½-hour private devotional time every day.

1 Corinthians 3:10

By the grace God has given me, I laid a foundation as a wise builder, and someone else is building on it. But each one should build with care.

9. FRAME

The strength of any man-made structure is its framework. This is true whether you are building a shed, a house or a skyscraper. It is the framework that bears the load of the walls and roof. It is the framework that gives the building strength and ensures that the building does not fall down. The framework for my shed is simple 2 × 4s because it is a small building. I have 2 × 4s in the floor, the walls and the roof trusses. You cannot see these until you go inside the shed. Then you can see what makes it strong.

In our Christian life, it's not what people see on the outside that makes us strong. Our spiritual strength comes from what is on the inside. What is holding you together as a Christian? What gives you spiritual strength? We can appear strong to people around us, but appearance is only on the outside. Unless we are strong in our faith on the inside, unless we are spiritually secure, we will not stand up to the winds of adversity. Strive to be strong from within.

ISAIAH 41:10

So do not fear, for I am with you;
  do not be dismayed, for I am your God.
  I will strengthen you and help you;
  I will uphold you with my righteous right hand.

10. WALLS

The whole purpose of a shed is to create an enclosure into which you put things that you want to keep safe and secure. The only way to do this is to build walls. Walls provide protection from the elements. Walls hide things from prying eyes. Walls discourage thieves. After I laid the foundation and the floor, my next step was to make and erect the walls. For this I selected straight (not warped) 2 × 4s from my stack of used lumber and overlaid this with ½-inch plywood sheeting. With the help of my crew (by now my wife, daughter and son-in-law had all volunteered to assist), I quickly had the walls up.

In our spiritual life, we are protected by the Spirit of God. The Bible says, "the LORD surrounds his people both now and forevermore" (Psalm 125:2). As the walls of my shed surround the things inside, so God surrounds those who trust in Him, shielding them from the devil's attacks and from temptations of the flesh. In Christ we are safe forevermore.

PSALM 139:5–6

You hem me in behind and before,
   and you lay your hand upon me.
   Such knowledge is too wonderful for me,
   too lofty for me to attain.

11. ROOF

L ike the walls of the shed, the roof is there to protect the contents of the shed from the elements. The roof trusses have to be sturdy. They have to stand up to wind and to hold up the weight of sheeting and shingles, along with snow if you live in the northern parts of the continent. They also have to be able to hold you up when you go on the roof to carry out repairs. I built the trusses in my driveway using 2 × 4s fastened together with plywood gussets that I made myself. After making the first truss, I used this as a pattern for the rest so that they all came out the same. In the end, I think I came out with a pretty solid roof.

In our Christian life it is a great encouragement to know that God is our strong protector. He not only surrounds us on each side but He also covers us. The Bible often refers to God as our shield and our strong tower. In one place there is a reference to the helmet of salvation. God is our protection against the spiritual forces of evil, against bad thoughts and sinful temptations. When times are difficult, look up and be assured that the Almighty is your strong protection.

PSALM 91:4

He will cover you with his feathers, and under his wings you will find refuge; his faithfulness will be your shield and rampart.

12. Shingles

Roof shingles serve two purposes, the main one being to protect the roof from the weather. Rain, hail and snow can do a lot of damage. Shingles are the shield against the elements. Their other purpose is to make the shed look good. I chose asphalt shingles for my shed because they are tough, economical and look pretty good as well. If you ask at your local building supply store for bundles that are broken open, you may get them at half price (I did). The shingles are fine; it's just the plastic wrap that is broken. The shingles go on the roof in layers overlapping one another. They are fastened to the roof with roofing nails.

In every life, some rain must fall. Often some hail, and snow as well. This is true of the Christian life as it is of any life. The Bible says that God "causes his sun to rise on the evil and the good, and sends rain on the righteous and the unrighteous" (Matthew 5:45). We are not going to be exempt from bad things happening to us just because we are Christians. But we can have the assurance that these things will not ruin us. Like the shingles on a shed, God is above us, protecting us from spiritual harm and guaranteeing our eternal salvation.

2 Corinthians 4:8, 9 (MEV)

We are troubled on every side, yet not distressed; we are perplexed, but not in despair;

Persecuted, but not forsaken; cast down, but not destroyed...

13. Door

A shed without a secure door is pretty much useless. Such a shed may protect from the weather some of the time, depending which way the wind is blowing; it will provide no protection at all from thieves or from prying eyes. A good, secure door is a must. The design plans for my shed called for double doors made of plywood, framed with 2 × 4s and hung with strong hinges. There were also some decorative elements to the doors. After the doors were put in place, I installed a latch mechanism with a padlock and key.

In the Bible, Jesus calls Himself "the Door" (John 10:1–18, KJV). He did not use the analogy of a shed, but that of a sheepfold. But the idea is the same. As "the Door," Jesus is the way into God's blessings. He will keep out thieves and robbers and all who intend to do us harm, but He will allow in those who follow God's way. In the culture of the Middle East in that time in history, a shepherd would lie across the opening to the sheep pen and literally become the gate (or the "door") to the sheep pen. No thief or wild animal could hurt the sheep without encountering the shepherd. As a Christian, you are one of God's flock. Jesus is the door that will protect you.

JOHN 10:9 (KJV)

I am the door: by me if any man enter in, he shall be saved, and shall go in and out, and find pasture.

14. Paint

My shed was starting to look like a shed. The floor and walls were up and the roof and shingles were in place. It was time to paint. Being the cheap guy I am, I went to the Restore, which is operated by Habitat for Humanity, and bought a gallon of paint (at half its original price) that had been donated by a construction company. Paint makes things look good, but it is more than that. Paint protects. And I wanted to get my plywood sheeting protected from the rain as quickly as possible. Paint also covers up things you don't want noticed, things like nail heads, scratches in the wood and knots. When people look at my shed, the first thing they notice is the paint. It is the paint that makes the first impression.

In our Christian life, people will first notice what is obvious about us. They will be impressed or unimpressed by what they immediately see—how we dress, how we walk, whether or not we smile. They will also be impressed or unimpressed by what they hear from us—whether our language is offensive or encouraging. As they get to know us more they will judge us even more by the things we do—how we show our love for others, our attitude and our work habits. These outward things are like paint on a shed—if they are good things, they will make a great first impression and cover up the minor flaws in our character.

1 Peter 4:8

Above all, love each other deeply, because love covers over a multitude of sins.

15. Trim

By this time in my construction project, my shed is fully functional. It has a solid foundation and floor, sturdy sides and a strong roof. The shingles are laid, the paint is on and the doors are hung. However, there is still one thing needed, and that is the trim.  The trim is that decorative board that runs along the edges of the walls. It does not add much to the functionality of the shed, other than cover up a seam or two that otherwise would have a small gap. The trim sets the shed apart, makes it look its best. The trim takes away the plainness of the shed and makes it look more attractive. After all, it is something my wife and I have to look at every day.

It is also important for Christians to look good. This is true first of all in the spiritual and moral sense. Our personalities and our character have to be attractive. Our attitude has to be positive. Our words have to be encouraging. We have to show to the world the beauty of Jesus. Someone said, "It is not enough to *be* righteous. We also have to appear righteous." What do your actions say about you? The other aspect is our physical appearance. While there is no official dress code for Christians, in whatever culture we live there is a cultural dress code that makes a statement to people around us. How we dress, how we look, even how we smell says something about us. What does your physical appearance say about you?

MATTHEW 5:16

Let your light shine before others, that they may see your good deeds and glorify your Father in heaven.

16. ORGANIZE

My shed was now complete. It was time to put it to use. The next stage was to organize the inside. I had plans for shelving, but winter was coming on and I had to get my lawnmower, pick, shovels, rakes, outboard motor and gas cans out of my garage to make room for my van. I also had to store my patio furniture. I confess there was not time to build shelves that first year. Everything went into the shed in a jumble. I put the padlock on, and there it all stayed safe, secure and unorganized until spring. Then it was clean-out time and the task of building shelves and reorganizing the contents.

I sometimes find that my Christian life is a little like that. A jumble of activities. I get in pretty much everything that should be in, but sometimes it is not very organized. There is worship at church, and private devotions, prayer, Bible reading, volunteer work, visiting the sick and donating to charity. The challenge for me is to get my life organized, to create a balance and a routine. And there is the danger of trying to cram too much into our lives as well. Let us remember to take one day at a time, to plan carefully and to let God direct our living.

PROVERBS 16:3

Commit to the LORD whatever you do, and he will establish your plans.

17. Mistakes

As much as I like my shed, it is not perfect. I made a few mistakes along the way. And some are obvious in the pictures, as some of you have no doubt observed. The first—and perhaps biggest—mistake was to try to save building material by putting the side sheeting on horizontally instead of vertically. This created a seam that is not on any framing. Consequently, this can allow water to get in when the rain is accompanied  by a strong wind. I will have to fix this with sealant. The other obvious mistake was to make my door too low. I keep hitting my head when coming out. I'm not so sure this can be fixed. But I have learned from these mistakes…so my next shed will be even better!

The lesson in life is as obvious as the mistakes in my shed. We do not live perfect lives. We make mistakes. We sometimes sin. We sometimes do and say things that are wrong. But that does not mean that our lives are thereby ruined. We can learn from those mistakes and those wrong choices. Some things we can fix. Some things we can't. But we can determine to build a better tomorrow than a yesterday. We can decide not to repeat that sin, but to repent of it and to get on with our lives as God directs.

1 John 1:9

If we confess our sins, he is faithful and just and will forgive us our sins and purify us from all unrighteousness.

18. IMPROVE

My shed has taught me a lot of things. Since starting this project I've learned how to use some of my power tools that had been collector items. I've learned some new carpentry skills. I've learned new vocabulary. And I've learned some things about myself, particularly that I am capable of building something without ending up in the hospital. But there is always room for improvement. My wife wants me to put in a window and make a window box for flowers. I'm thinking of putting some kind of decorative piece for the gable over the door.

As Christians we are constantly growing in our faith. We are growing in Christ-likeness. It is God's plan that we become more and more like Jesus as we progress. The Bible says that we are God's temple. A temple is a whole lot more elaborate than a shed. God lives in you, if you are a Christian. But you are not yet perfect. There is always room for improvement. And God is not finished with you yet. God works with us to make these daily improvements. It is our responsibility to work with Him.

COLOSSIANS 1:10

live a life worthy of the Lord and please him in every way: bearing fruit in every good work, growing in the knowledge of God,

19. ENJOY

The Bible says that God created the heavens and the earth and everything in them in six days (whether literally or figuratively, it doesn't matter). God then looked at what He had made and declared it to be "very good." And then God rested from His work of creation. God did not rest because He was tired; He rested to enjoy His creation.

Now that I have finished my shed, I sometimes sit on my back deck and admire my creation. I say to my wife, "That's not a bad-looking shed."

And she says, "It's a good shed, Fred."

And I say, "Yes, that's exactly what it is. It's a Fred Shed."

And we both laugh.

And when winter sets in I know that all my summer stuff is safe and secure, cuddled together in my Fred Shed, waiting for spring, and I am well pleased.

Christians, of all people, should appreciate and enjoy God's creative work. This includes both the world around us and God's work within us. Artists and poets are probably closest to appreciating the beauty of God's creation. Farmers and those who work with wild things—fishermen, hunters, ranchers and naturalists—also appreciate God's creation. People whose work is helping others probably appreciate God's design in humanity more than anyone—doctors, nurses, teachers, clergy and humanitarians. In addition to appreciating the Creation, let us also give thanks to the Creator. He is well pleased with everything He has made.

REVELATION 4:11

"You are worthy, our Lord and God, to receive glory and honour and power, for you created all things, and by your will they were created and have their being."

20. Help

My shed is built, now what do I do? The answer: help another guy (in this case, my son) build his shed. It is true that building one shed does not make a person an expert in shed building. However, experience counts for something. At the very least, I can point out some of the mistakes I made along the way so that my fellow shed-builder won't make the same ones. And at best, I can pitch in and lend a hand. After all, I now know how to use a table saw, a mitre saw and a power drill, not to mention my hammer and handsaw. Helping others gives as much satisfaction as building your own shed.

Christianity has always been a religion of "others." It is about helping others, encouraging others, carrying the burdens of others. William and Catherine Booth, the founders of the Salvation Army, dedicated their whole adult lives to helping the poor and marginalized in society. Mother Theresa, a Roman Catholic nun, was world-renowned for her work with the downtrodden of India. Jesus, our Saviour, said, "For even the Son of Man did not come to be served, but to serve, and to give his life as a ransom for many" (Mark 10:45). As followers of Christ, let us help others build a better life for themselves in His name.

JOHN 13:15

I have set you an example that you should do as I have done for you.

Questions for Reflection and Discussion

1. How does a man know God's plan for his life?

2. What are man's roll and God's roll in building a life?

3. What do we do about our past mistakes?

4. What are some of the lessons you've learned as you built your life?

5. How important is planning?

6. Why should a man seek to know God's will for him?

7. What advice would you give a young man starting out in life?

PART 2

GARDENS

1. Seeds

Today we begin a series of thoughts I gleaned from the backyard vegetable garden and the front yard flower garden that my wife and I planted. I figure that the flower garden is hers, but the vegetable garden is mine, but she might argue with that. Our first task was to decide what to plant. Way back  in the fall, Shirley said she wanted tulips and crocuses coming up in the spring, so it was off to the store to purchase bulbs. With cold weather approaching and snow falling in some parts of the country, we buried bulbs in anticipation for spring that was six months away. I said I wanted to plant vegetables in the backyard and dreamt of carrots, turnips, tomatoes and perhaps potatoes. But I would have to wait until spring to make my selection and begin planting. The spring would also reveal whether the bulbs we sowed would grow.

> An old gospel song says,
> "Seeds now we are sowing, and fruit they must bear,
> For blessing or cursing, for joy or despair;
> Though we may forget them, the things of the past
> Will work out God's sentence upon us at last."

God has given us the power to decide what "seeds" we want to plant in our life. These can be seeds of bitterness, hatred, resentment and the like, or they can be seeds of thankfulness, love, forgiveness and joy. The choice is ours, so let us examine our lives daily and decide well what we want to grow in our lives.

Galatians 6:7–8

A man reaps what he sows. Whoever sows to please their flesh, from the flesh will reap destruction; whoever sows to please the Spirit, from the Spirit will reap eternal life.

2. Location

Once my wife and I had decided what we wanted to grow, the next big decision was where. There were already two flower beds of sorts at the front of our house (we had just recently moved here), so we thought it best to utilize these rather than dig up our lawn. The bulbs in the fall and plants in the spring would go at the front of the house. The backyard had a few scraggy plants in one corner that seemed out of place. This would be our vegetable garden. We transplanted a bush to the front of the house and two perennials to one of the flower beds. The bulbs, bushes and vegetables had no say in where they were put. Their responsibility was simply to bloom where they were planted.

While we often have choices in life, sometimes there are circumstances that restrict or eliminate choice. An illness may force us to retire early. It is not our choice. The company we work for closes and we are forced to look for work elsewhere. It is not our choice. A flood destroys our neighbourhood and we are forced to relocate. It is not our choice. Our spouse dies and we are forced to make decisions about our future. Sometimes we are uprooted. Sometimes we are like plants growing in rocky soil, struggling to make a living. In situations beyond our control, we have to learn to trust God completely and to bloom where circumstances have planted us.

Philippians 4:12

I know what it is to be in need, and I know what it is to have plenty. I have learned the secret of being content in any and every situation, whether well fed or hungry, whether living in plenty or in want. I can do all this through him who gives me strength.

3. Preparation

We decided what to plant and where, but we couldn't just scatter the seeds on the ground. Nor could we just dig holes and put the bulbs in. We first had to prepare the ground for planting. For the backyard vegetable garden this meant removing several large, flat patio-type stones and levelling parts of the ground. For the front yard flower garden this meant digging up a lot of ground cover that was choking up everything else. On both sites the ground had to be broken up and made workable. We also added ten bags of topsoil to the sites.

Sometimes in our eagerness to witness for Jesus, we forget to prepare the soil before we plant the seeds. By that I mean that sometimes Christians begin to testify about their faith to people who are not yet ready to listen or who don't even know the vocabulary that the Christian is using. Before we can begin to plant the seeds of faith in the lives of others, we first have to build trust and let the other person see that we are real and that we care for them. We may have to remove obstacles to faith such as negative conceptions and a judgmental attitude. We may have to create more level ground between "us and them." We may have to add something to our relationships before we can plant those seeds.

Matthew 9:10

While Jesus was having dinner at Matthew's house, many tax collectors and sinners came and ate with him and his disciples.

4. Flowers

Flowers are associated with beauty and attractiveness, which is why my wife is in charge of the flower garden. That is not to say that I am uninterested. It was I who had to dig out all the old ground cover and spread and mix new topsoil into the garden. But she had the final say as to what flowers to purchase, and it was a joint decision as to how these were arranged in the garden. Flowers add colour to our front yard and create curb appeal. They make our property more attractive and inspire admiration. Our yard would definitely be less inviting if we did not have flowers.

Where are the "flowers" in your life? By that I mean, what is it about your life that is attractive? And I don't mean just your physical appearance, although that, too, can be attractive. But there are others things that can attract people to one another. Things that we do—smiling, offering a friendly handshake, assisting a neighbour, volunteering at a church. Things that we say—words of encouragement, giving praise, complimenting your spouse. Your life as a Christian can attract people to the Lord if you strive to be like Jesus in all you do and say.

Philippians 2:15

become blameless and pure, "children of God without fault in a warped and crooked generation." Then you will shine among them like stars in the sky

5. Vegetables

Vegetables are practical plants. They are necessary for life and health. Growing your own can save you money, which may be the real reason I wanted to grow them instead of flowers. The truth is that both my wife and I like the idea of going to our vegetable patch and harvesting our own home-grown food. We chose mostly root crops—carrots, beets, turnip and radishes—but also some veggies on the vine, like tomatoes and beans. And some green onions and lettuce, which I don't know how to classify. It was sheer delight for the both of us when we harvested our first radishes and lettuce for a salad after only a few weeks.

Perhaps you would like your Christian life to be all roses and tulips, full of colour and pleasure. While those days will come, there is also a practical side— the vegetable side— to our faith. Enjoying pot-luck suppers at church, dancing to praise-and-worship songs and watching kids perform in a biblical drama are the flowery parts of the Christian life. The real meat and potatoes parts of our faith are the day-to-day things that build us up spiritually. These are things like daily prayer and meditation on the word of God, participating in a serious Bible study group and being part of a Christian ministry team. Enjoy the flowers, but don't pass over the vegetables.

James 1:22

Do not merely listen to the word, and so deceive yourselves. Do what it says.

6. Plant

We'd decided what to plant and where. We'd prepared the ground and purchased seeds for the vegetable garden and plants from the nursery for the flower garden. Now it was time to plant. We started with the flower garden. We sorted out the tiny flower plants and laid them on the ground to create a pattern of colours that we thought would look good. Then we dug shallow holes in the earth and carefully placed each individual plant into its place. When finished, it looked very promising. For the vegetable garden we dug shallow trenches and filled each one with seeds. A row of carrots here, a row of beans there and so on. Then we covered the seeds with a shallow layer of soil. When finished all we could see was a flat area of soil…and a lot of hope in our heart. We also put in some tomato and rhubarb plants and a raspberry bush.

Christian witnessing and evangelism have often been described as planting seeds. In fact, Jesus compared himself to a farmer who was scattering seeds on his land. Although not all the seeds would germinate, take root and produce a crop, some would. For that reason, the farmer did not lose heart. Jesus planted seeds of faith as He preached the gospel and ministered to people. One of our responsibilities as Christians is to plant seeds of faith as Jesus did. Plant in hope.

Mark 4:3, 8

"Listen! A farmer went out to sow his seed. ⁴ As he was scattering the seed, some fell… on good soil.

7. TRANSPLANT

I n the course of planting our vegetable garden, it was necessary for me to transplant two perennials and a bush. The bush was in the corner and tended to spread out onto the garden area. The perennials were in the middle of the ground where I wanted to plant vegetables. With a great deal  of digging and a lot of grunting, I managed to uproot the bush and transport it to the front of the house where it covered a bare spot. Moving the two perennials was easier. These went into a garden of perennials to the side of our property. Now everything was where it was supposed to be for the purposes we intended.

During our more than twenty years as pastors, my wife and I were often "transplanted" from one community to another. Like those plants in my garden, we did not have any say in the matter but we put down roots and did our best to do our duty in each new place we lived. In your life, too, there will be times when you will be transplanted, sometimes by your own choice and sometimes by circumstances out of your control. It is wise to remember in such times that God is the Divine Gardener, and although decisions seem to be made arbitrarily by others, God's purposes for us will work out in the end.

PSALM 1:1–3

Blessed is the one…whose delight is in the law of the Lord
That person is like a tree planted by streams of water,
which yields its fruit in season
and whose leaf does not wither—
whatever they do prospers.

8. WATER

Water is the lifeblood of plants. Without water ground becomes a desert, plants shrivel and die, crops fail. Once we had our seeds in the ground we had to make sure that we watered the soil daily and continued to do so after the young shoots appeared. In fact, watering was something we had to do throughout the entire growing season. Sometimes rain came and the plants were watered naturally, but with the hot, dry summer we experienced we had to do the watering ourselves most of the time.

In the Bible water is a powerful symbol used in various ways. The Holy Spirit is symbolized as water being poured out upon God's people and being poured into our hearts. In that instance God is the one who is watering our souls. Water is also used to symbolize the care that Christians give to one another. Through their encouraging words and uplifting attitude they refresh each other's souls. As a Christian you need both God's Holy Spirit filling you daily and the support of other Christians to encourage you. Seek to be spiritually refreshed each day and find ways to refresh others.

1 CORINTHIANS 3:6

I planted the seed, Apollos watered it, but God has been making it grow

9. CARE

Almost every day after planting seeds in our vegetable garden, my wife Shirley and I would check the ground to see if anything was growing. It seemed to take forever before anything green poked through the earth. And then one day it happened. Shirley came running to me shouting, "Something is grown in our garden!" I checked, and sure enough, a row of little green shoots was peeking through the ground…and then another…and another. Our garden had begun! It was now our responsibility to care for these tender shoots and help them to grow.

In your life, too, there are probably "little green shoots." By that I mean people who are new to the faith, people who have only recently begun a relationship with Jesus. They may be older in years, but as Christians they are "babes in Christ." Or there may be children in your life, whether part of your family or your friends' families. They are also tender shoots, even if they don't yet know Jesus. If God has placed such people in your life it is because God expects you to help with nurturing them. Do all you can to help these "little ones" to grow in their relationship with the Lord.

MARK 10:14

He said to them, "Let the little children come to me, and do not hinder them, for the kingdom of God belongs to such as these.

10. Weeds

It was not long after the vegetable shoots came through the ground that weeds also began to appear. In fact, in some cases they appeared at the same time so that it was hard at first to tell which was a weed and which was the vegetable plant. So we had to let both grow until we could identify which was the weed and which was the vegetable. After a while it became obvious which was which and we then dutifully extracted the weed. But they never gave up easily and kept coming back all summer long so that it was a constant battle to keep an eye out for them and to keep removing them.

The lesson here for us Christians is obvious. The weeds in our life are those things that should not be there. They are the things that choke our faith and hinder our spiritual growth. These "weeds" are things like bad habits—watching too much TV, being overly involved in sports, having a negative attitude, grumbling, laziness and the like. The "weeds" can be sins—addiction to alcohol, drugs or porn; telling lies, gossiping, deceitfulness. Whatever hinders our spiritual progress is a weed and needs to be removed.

LUKE 8:14

The seed that fell among thorns stands for those who hear, but as they go on their way they are choked by life's worries, riches and pleasures, and they do not mature.

11. Rabbits

Both our vegetable garden and our flower garden were doing well. In early spring the crocus shoots peeked through the ground. Shortly afterwards they began to disappear before developing blooms. I took a close look and discovered the shoots had been bitten off. Then early one morning I caught sight of the thief. A rabbit from the park across the road. Two months later when we planted our vegetable garden, I had forgotten about the rabbit, and when the vegetable shoots began coming through the ground my carrot, lettuce and beet shoots began disappearing. Then I caught sight of him (or her) again. The little varmint was persistent…I had a battle on my hands.

In our Christian life there are little things that eat away at our faith. If we are not careful these things will destroy or seriously damage our Christian witness. In a previous generation, Sunday school children would sing a somewhat silly song with a thoughtful message: *"Root them out, get them gone; all the little bunnies in the field of corn. Envy, jealousy, malice, pride; they must never in my heart abide."*

As your faith begins to grow, be aware of the little things that may rob you of your joy and peace. And do all you can to protect yourself from these spiritual predators.

Song of Solomon 2:15

Catch for us the foxes, the little foxes that ruin the vineyards,
our vineyards that are in bloom.

12. PROTECT

Once I discovered that rabbits were eating the shoots of my vegetables before they had a chance to develop, I had to figure out how to protect my crop. The solution was to build wooden garden boxes with mesh top to keep the critters out. It took some time and effort and a little financial investment, but I eventually built two critter-proof boxes that provided a safe environment for my little crop. The tops of the boxes could be removed for weeding and thinning.

If we find that our faith is slipping or we feel that we are not as close to the Lord as we once were, we need to determine why. Then we need to do something about it. We need to protect ourselves from whatever is drawing us away from God. The Bible talks about putting on the armour of God, using the shield of faith and the sword of the Spirit, which is the word of God. There are things we can do to protect ourselves spiritually. Things like developing a healthy devotional life, participating in a good Bible study group and worshipping regularly at your church.

EPHESIANS 6:11

Put on the full armor of God, so that you can take your stand against the devil's schemes.

13. Fertilize

I rescued my vegetables from the rabbits and built boxes around the plants to protect them. But they still needed one more thing: food. The soil where I planted my vegetables was not the greatest. It needed improvement. I went to the garden supply centre and bought ten bags of topsoil, rich in plant nutrients. Carefully I mixed this into the soil in the boxes, thus creating a healthy environment for my crop. I then bought fertilizer that I mixed with water and weekly poured this life-boosting food into my garden.

Sometimes you can't do much about where you live and where you work. If your home environment is rich in a heritage of faith, a place where people encourage one another and forgive one another and pray for one another, then you have a healthy spiritual environment. If your workplace is one where you can interact with your colleagues in a friendly, non-threatening way and perhaps at times even talk about your faith, you have a lot going for you. But if your home or workplace is not like that, don't despair. Find ways to enrich your spiritual life through your church and Christian friends. Then you can be the one to make life richer for others who as yet do not believe.

1 Thessalonians 5:11

Therefore encourage one another and build each other up, just as in fact you are doing.

14. REPLANT

Because of the damage that the rabbits did to my vegetable garden, I lost all my lettuce and some of my carrots and beets. Several weeks of the growing season were past, but I figured if the weather stayed warm there was still a good chance to replant. So although it was late for planting, I once again put seeds into the ground and started over. This time the seeds were secure in their protected boxes.

It is not always easy to start over, but it is not impossible. If after you began your Christian journey something happened to diminish your faith or interrupt your walk with God, don't despair. It is never too late to start over. Our God is the God of second chances. You can rework the soil. You can plant the seeds of faith again. You can produce a crop for the Lord. In the Bible many of God's children started over after failing the first time. Among them are Moses, Jonah and Peter, to name just three. There is yet a promising future for those willing to try again.

JONAH 3:1–3

Then the word of the Lord came to Jonah a second time: "Go to the great city of Nineveh and proclaim to it the message I give you."
Jonah obeyed the word of the Lord and went to Nineveh.

15. SUPPORT

Besides planting seeds in my garden, I also put in about a dozen tomato plants. They were small, fragile things that I bought from a local nursery. I put them in with hope that someday they would produce fruit. In anticipation of this and as a sign of my faith in nature, I bought a tomato cage for each of the plants to give them support as they grew. The plants were about four inches high, and the cages were about three feet high. They would have a lot of growing to do, but they would be surrounded by a support system as they developed.

Perhaps in your life there are new Christians or children who are just learning about Jesus. Their faith is small. Their understanding of the Christian life is very limited. As they start on their journey with God they need the support of Christians who are older and more mature than they are. They need help to remain upright in their life. You can be that support. You can be part of the church team or the network of friends who help others to grow in their faith.

GALATIANS 6:2

Carry each other's burdens, and in this way you will fulfill the law of Christ.

16. Butterflies

I was having lunch with my wife on our back deck when we noticed colourful, dancing butterflies flittering among the turnip leaves. The dusty white wings of some of them reflected the sunlight and they added a contrasting colour to the green of the turnip tops. Their erratic behaviour fascinated us and we smiled at the dancing insects. What we did not realize was that while we watched and smiled, those tiny insects with their hypnotic dance were depositing hundreds of eggs on our vegetable leaves. A short time later the eggs hatched into larvae, which promptly began eating holes in the turnip leaves. As the larvae grew so did the damage to the plants. Large holes and brown deposits on the leaves nearly killed the turnips.

There is always the danger of letting into our lives little things which appear harmless, but which can grow to the point where our Christian life will deteriorate. For some it may be the "harmless" flirtation with someone in the office. The teasing and friendly banter become romance and grow into an affair that can destroy a family. For others it may be a "harmless" alcoholic drink at lunch each day. The one drink grows to two and then to three until the person suddenly realizes they have a drinking problem. We must constantly assess our actions and take the necessary steps to keep ourselves in line.

1 Corinthians 9:27 (NKJV)

But I discipline my body and bring it into subjection, lest, when I have preached to others, I myself should become disqualified.

17. Thinning

One of the most difficult lessons from my garden was that of thinning the plants. The instructions on the seed packets said to sow liberally, then after the plants began to grow to thin out the weaker ones so that the stronger plants would not be crowded out. To uproot plants that were quite healthy and were doing what they were designed to do was difficult. I felt sorry for them because they were being uprooted for no reason of their own. I had to learn not to be so sentimental about my plants.

In our Christian life we can sometimes be so eager to serve the Lord and the Church that we crowd our life with too many good things. As a result, nothing that we do amounts to much. It is better to do a few things well than to do many things shoddily. If we try to do too much too quickly, the result is that very little gets done properly. And we can get burnt out. We need to weed out some things so we can do those things that we do best. No one can do everything. Don't feel guilty because you have to say no to some things. Concentrate on using the gifts God has given you.

Romans 12:6–7

We have different gifts, according to the grace given to each of us. If your gift is prophesying, then prophesy in accordance with your faith; if it is serving, then serve; if it is teaching, then teach;

18. GROUNDHOGS

 When tomatoes began appearing on the tomato plants and our garden was getting green, my wife and I thought it would be nice to encourage birds to come around. We bought a bird feeder and a bag of birdseed and placed this near the garden. As we usually ate breakfast on our back deck, we imagined colourful songbirds chirping around us. Well, things did not turn out quite like that. Mostly we attracted crows, starlings and blackbirds that drove the smaller birds away. And then came the granddaddy of groundhogs. He ate the birdseed that fell on the ground and then started on our tomatoes, stealing the fruit before we could harvest it. We took down the bird feeder. After a few mornings of getting sprayed with the water hose the groundhog eventually left.

In the old days the veteran Christians would sometimes talk about the devil stealing their blessing. By that they meant that after they had had a great blessing, perhaps at a revival meeting, a few days later things would go wrong and they would get upset and discouraged. In your Christian life, don't let anyone or anything steal your blessing. Don't let the devil rob you of your joy. Don't let anything spoil the fruit that the Spirit is cultivating in your life.

1 PETER 5:8

Be alert and of sober mind. Your enemy the devil prowls around like a roaring lion looking for someone to devour.

19. FAILURES

Despite our best efforts, not everything we planted grew. Some things grew well. The tomato plants produced tomatoes. The bean plants produced beans. The beet plants produced beets. But some things just never grew. I could not blame it on the rabbits or the groundhog. I treated every plant alike, watering and feeding them. For example, I planted a little spruce tree, put fertilizer underneath it and carefully watered it every day. But despite my best efforts it died. So did some of my turnip plants and all of my asparagus. But I was thankful for those that did grow.

In your life not everything you attempt to do for the Lord will succeed. You do your best to plant seeds of faith in the hearts of children in your life. Some grow up to be preachers. Some grow up to be prostitutes. You did your best. You witness to your friends and neighbours. Some come to faith. Some do not. You volunteer at your church or favourite charity and your project fails. You start an outreach program and it does not work. But some things that you do will work. Some things will grow. Be thankful for those that do.

MARK 4:7, 8

Other seed fell among thorns, which grew up and choked the plants, so that they did not bear grain. Still other seed fell on good soil. It came up, grew and produced a crop, some multiplying thirty, some sixty, some a hundred times.

20. HARVEST

The final lesson from my garden is to enjoy and share the harvest. As summer began to draw to a close the tomatoes began turning red, the beans were growing bigger, and the beets were rising from the earth. At least once a week we gathered something from our garden—greens from our turnip tops and beets, onions for our salad, and beans. When visitors came we liked to serve them something fresh from the garden. It was a delight to enjoy and to share with others the harvest from our backyard garden.

All of us have been blessed in many ways. These blessings are not just for ourselves. God has blessed us so that we can bless others. If God has given you money, share it with those who have none. If God has given you a house, invite others to come and visit. If God has given you a talent, use it to serve others. If you have an education or a car or good health, enjoy it and share your blessings with others. The essence of Christianity is loving God through loving other people. God will reward those who share.

MATTHEW 25:40

Truly I tell you, whatever you did for one of the least of these brothers and sisters of mine, you did for me.

Questions for Reflection and Discussion

1. Identify some good seeds and some bad seeds in a man's life.

2. What can you do to encourage the growth of good seeds in your life?

3. How can a man bloom where he is planted?

4. What things can eat away our faith and what can we do about this?

5. How can you support a weaker brother?

6. How can a man handle failure?

7. How can a man share his blessings with others?

PART 3

BOATS

1. Types

Over the years, I have ridden in, borrowed, rented and owned a number of different types of boats. I recall rowboats, and a small punt, both of which I rowed to get anywhere. Needless to say I did not go far in these. There was also a canoe, which required almost as much work as the rowboats. Then there were several small aluminium fishing boats to which I could attach an outboard motor. More fun than a rowboat, and I could go farther. And then there were the sailboats. More fun than the aluminium boats, and I could stay out overnight and even cook on board. But each boat had a purpose. How boring and impractical life on the water would be if every boat were alike.

The same is true of our lives. We are all different from each other. Each of us has talents and abilities unique to us. We each have different personalities, different looks and different temperaments. It would be as unfair to compare ourselves with others as it would be to compare a canoe to a sailboat. As there are different types of boats; there are different kinds of people. We should not expect others to be like us. And we should not try to be like others. We should learn to appreciate ourselves as part of God's Creation and seek to find our purpose and place in life.

1 Corinthians 12:6

There are different kinds of working, but in all of them and in everyone it is the same God at work.

2. BOATERS

Depending on where you live and the size of your boat, you may or may not need a boat licence. However, before you venture out on the water it is a good idea to study the regulations and safety protocols relating to the watercraft you are going to use. There are online courses that teach boating safety, but they do not teach you how to use the particular boat you have. For that you need to actually get out on the water. For those of us who use a sailboat, there are special skills and specific information about wind and waves that need to be learned. I took thirteen weeks of in-class instructions, several days of hands-on instructions from a sailing club and the help of an experienced sailor to get me to the point of feeling confident about my own sailing. Learn from other boaters. Ask questions. You'll find they are eager to pass on what they know.

In our Christian life we need good teaching and reliable coaching if we are to grow in our faith and become the Christians we ought to be. I am very grateful to the Sunday school teachers and youth Bible leaders I had in my formative years, and to the various pastors who led our small church. I am thankful for the opportunity of taking courses at a Bible college. And today I am still a part of a home Bible study group. We can try to "go it alone" as a Christian, but this often results in misinterpretations of Scripture and a Christian life that is not well balanced. To be the best we can be, we need to keep learning from each other as we seek to apply God's word to our lives.

COLOSSIANS 3:16 (NKJV)

Let the word of Christ dwell in you richly in all wisdom, teaching and admonishing one another in psalms and hymns and spiritual songs, singing with grace in your hearts to the Lord.

3. EXPERIENCE

There are two kinds of learning experiences—book learning and hands-on learning. To learn how to sail, I needed both. Book learning taught me the rules of navigation, the names of the different parts of the sailboat, what the different sails and lines were used for, how to read a chart and  a whole lot more useful information. Hands-on learning enabled me to develop a skill that I did not possess before. I learned to hoist the sails, set the sails, sail using a compass and to feel confident about my boat and myself. I learned not to panic when the boat heeled (tipped to the side). I learned to tack to windward and a whole lot more that can only be learned by doing.

In our Christian life we also need book learning and hands-on learning. The book of course is the Bible. This needs to be our primary source of learning. We can supplement this with reading from commentaries, inspirational books, devotional books and biographies of great Christians. We also need hands-on learning to develop skills of serving, helping, encouraging, witnessing—even preaching and teaching. The Christian life is not meant to be lived in your head; it is to be lived among others as you demonstrate your Christ-like qualities to those around you.

2 PETER 1:5–8

...make every effort to add to your faith goodness; and to goodness, knowledge; and to knowledge, self-control; and to self-control, perseverance; and to perseverance, godliness; and to godliness, mutual affection; and to mutual affection, love. For if you possess these qualities in increasing measure, they will keep you from being ineffective and unproductive in your knowledge of our Lord Jesus Christ.

4. PURCHASE

Leaning about sailing is exciting. Actually sailing is fun and adventurous. But at some point, I had to actually purchase a boat of my own. There is only so much you can do in the classroom. And your friends will tolerate your sailing with them only so long. To be a genuine sailor, I not only needed to know how to sail but I also had to make a commitment and buy a boat. Fortunately, when it comes to good used boats, sailboats are relatively inexpensive. My first sailboat was a 20-ft Matilda design. I eventually sold that one and bought another 20-footer, a DS20 design, much roomier and a little faster. I could never know the real freedom of sailing without making that commitment.

The same is true in our Christian life. You can study the Bible, go to church and meet in a small group with Christian friends. But you will never know the saving grace of God until you make a commitment of your life to Christ. Neither the Bible nor the Church, nor your Christian friends can save you. Only Jesus can do that. To be a genuine Christian with a born-again experience you must make that personal commitment to Jesus.

LUKE 9:23

Then he said to them all: "Whoever wants to be my disciple must deny themselves and take up their cross daily and follow me

5. PORT

Having made a commitment and purchased a boat, my next big decision was where to put it. I could not simply park it on my driveway. It was not going to go anywhere there. Sailboats are not like powerboats—you can't simply launch them and take them out of the water every time you use them. You have to have a dock to tie them to for the season. And if you don't own a dock you have to rent one, usually at a marina. Putting my boat in a marina was another financial commitment, but it rewarded me with a sheltered harbour, a network of support from other sailors and times of fellowship and fun with other like-minded people.

As a Christian, you can't simply park yourself at home and sing, "I'm satisfied with Jesus here." You need to find a spiritual marina, a place where you can find a network of support from other Christians. A place where you can enjoy fellowship with other like-minded people who have also committed their lives to Jesus. You need to join a church where you can find shelter from life's storms and from where you can launch yourself into service. Look around and find the group that best meets your needs.

ACTS 2:46

Every day they continued to meet together in the temple courts. They broke bread in their homes and ate together with glad and sincere hearts...

6. MAST

The most prominent feature of a sailboat is the mast. This is a tall pole, usually made of aluminium, that rises from the deck. The mast supports the sail and the boom (a shorter pole attached to the underside of the sail). The mast has to be strong to support the force of the wind when it fills the sail. While the sail itself is light, the force of the wind can be tremendous in a strong breeze or gale. It is therefore extremely important for the mast and the system of stays and shrouds that support it to be strong.

In your Christian life also, you need a strong support system. The Christian life is not always easy, particularly if you are going to take your stand publicly. Your moral and ethical stand will sometimes clash with popular culture. Some people may be offended by your beliefs. Some decisions you make may cost you your job or deny you a promotion. Some of your friends may no longer associate with you. For all the winds of adversity you face, you will need the strong support system of other believers and your faith in Jesus to see you through.

JOSHUA 1:9

Have I not commanded you? Be strong and courageous. Do not be afraid; do not be discouraged, for the Lord your God will be with you wherever you go."

7. SAILS

S ails are what define a sailboat. People stand on the shore and look out at sailboats because of the sails. But sails do more than make a boat look good. They are essential for moving the boat through the water. They have a purpose. They act like the engine in a power boat, except that they draw their power from the wind. On most yachts you will see two sails: a large sail (called the mainsail) attached to a mast, and a smaller sail (called the foresail or jib) attached to a line at the front of the boat. The sails are what drive the boat. Without sails, a sailboat would go nowhere.

I like to think that the purpose of our life is like the sails on the sailboat. Without a purpose we will get nowhere. We will be driven by every wind and tide around us, by every popular belief and every fashionable activity. What is your life's mainsail? What do you consider the main reason you exist? What are your smaller goals? If you are to progress in your faith and life, you need to know your priorities and set your life's sails to those purposes.

GALATIANS 4:18

It is fine to be zealous, provided the purpose is good, and to be so always, not just when I am with you.

8. Keel

People who don't understand how sailboats work often wonder why yachts don't capsize when they lean over to the side. This leaning is called heeling. Small sailboats like a dingy do sometimes capsize, which is why you might see sailors leaning out over the side to try to prevent that. In a yacht with a crew of only one or two, it is not possible to keep the boat upright by moving the crew around. Yachts have a heavy counterweight built into their keel. This counterweight of concrete or steel balances the force of the wind in the sails so that the boat does not tip over.

What keeps you from going "bottom up" in your spiritual life? Winds of adversity will blow, have no doubt about that. There will be times when you will feel that you are about to lose control. There will be times when you will feel swamped. There will be times when you will feel that you are about to experience a "shipwreck." In such times remember what keeps your life in balance. It is that strong spiritual force that the world cannot see but that you know is there, keeping you in place. Instead of desperately trying to balance things yourself, rely on God's Holy Spirit. He will keep you on an even keel.

Proverbs 3:5 (KJV)

Trust in the Lord with all thine heart; and lean not unto thine own understanding.

9. Rudder

One of the most important parts of any boat is the rudder. This is a flat surface, usually made of aluminium or wood that is attached to the transom (back end) of the boat, directly behind the keel. Like the keel, the rudder is underwater and cannot be seen. Attached to the rudder is either a tiller (a kind of handle) or cables leading to a steering wheel. The rudder is the main control used for changing the direction of the boat. Compared to the size of the boat, the rudder is relatively small, but it is this small part that controls the entire boat.

It is extremely important for a Christian to be in control of their life. Nothing turns off unbelievers more quickly than a Christian who does not have self-control. A Christian who cannot control their tongue can cause a lot of damage. One who cannot control their appetite or sexual desires presents a poor example to others. On the other hand, a Christian who demonstrates self-control of their temper, and patience in the face of adversity, is a powerful witness of the power of Christ.

1 Thessalonians 4:4

...each of you should learn to control your own body in a way that is holy and honorable

10. LINES

On a sailboat ropes are called lines. Not all lines are the same. They vary in dimension and quality, depending on their use. The anchor line, for example, is often made of nylon or polyester and is usually thicker in diameter than the other lines on the boat. The lines used to trim the sails (that is, adjust them) are called sheets. Those used to hoist the sail are called halyards. These are usually made of Kevlar. Some ropes are stranded and others are braided. All lines are made of thin strands of yarn (some natural, some synthetic) that are twisted or braided together to make a strong rope.

Everyone knows that there is strength in numbers. Just as one strand of yarn is weak, so one person trying to live the Christian life in their own strength will find themselves weak. No one can live a powerful Christian life on their own. By ourselves we are weak. God never intended us to do this alone. He has promised to be with us, and He has put us in the community of believers. On our own we will break, but united with Jesus and in the company of other Christians we are strong.

ECCLESIASTES 4:12

Though one may be overpowered, two can defend themselves. A cord of three strands is not quickly broken

11. COMPASS

For centuries sailors have relied on their compass to find their way across vast stretches of unmarked ocean. When out of sight of land or sailing in a fog, there is no way to tell in which direction you are heading without a compass or GPS. A compass contains a magnet that lines up with the earth's magnetic pole. It is therefore possible to navigate fairly confidently even when you cannot see any onshore marks to guide you. On my sailboat the compass is mounted where I can easily see it while operating the tiller so that I can keep the boat on a steady course at all times.

Many old gospel songs have compared elements of our Christian faith to a compass. Some songs describe the Bible as a compass that points us in the right direction. Other songs talk of the Holy Spirit as our compass that guides us to Christ and Heaven. There are songs that refer to our conscience as a compass. All of these images have merit. But whether you talk about the Bible or the Holy Spirit or your conscience, all of them give direction only. The compass does not steer the boat. In the end it is up to you to decide the direction of your life. You can choose to ignore or to follow the directions that God gives you.

MATTHEW 9:9

As Jesus went on from there, he saw a man named Matthew sitting at the tax collector's booth. "Follow me," he told him, and Matthew got up and followed him.

12. Lights

One of the most important safety lessons for sailors is to make sure that other boaters are aware of their boat's presence. On a clear day most boats can easily be seen. At night it is a different story. This is why all boats have to be equipped with lights in the event that they are out after dark. The regulations vary according to the size of the boat, but most often boats have a green light showing on the starboard (right), a red light showing on the port (left) and a white light showing on the stern (back). On a sailboat, there is a white light at the top of the mast. In fog, boats have to sound a horn or bell.

In our post-modern, post-Christian culture, it is more important than ever for Christians to be seen and heard. Our Western culture is steadily growing darker. We need to let our light shine so that all who are around us will know who we are and what we are. We don't need to blast them out of the water with a giant floodlight. But neither should we hide our light. An unmistakable "red light" will make it clear where we draw the line. A "green light" will show what our standards are. And a "white light" will reveal our true self. And when things are morally foggy, let us not hesitate to make our voices heard.

JOHN 3:21

But whoever lives by the truth comes into the light, so that it may be seen plainly that what they have done has been done in the sight of God.

13. FENDERS

If you visit a marina you will often see cylindrical rubber devices hanging from the sides of boats that are docked. These are not decorations (they are too tacky looking for that). These rubber cylinders are called fenders or bumpers, depending on which part of the world you live. Their purpose is to protect the side of the boat from damage that might be caused by rubbing against the dock or another boat. Fenders don't protect from serious collisions but from day-to-day interaction with the environment of a marina.

In our Christian life we have to live and interact with other people. Some of them are Christian, others are not. Most of the time these people will not cause us wilful damage. However, the accumulative effect of day-to-day interaction with others who might rub us the wrong way can sometimes get us down. To cushion the negative effect caused by the hurtful actions and words of others we need to have spiritual fenders. We need to be able to lessen the impact with our own soft words, kind actions and quiet demeanour. In this way we avoid hurt feelings and damaged relationships.

PROVERBS 15:1

A gentle answer turns away wrath, but a harsh word stirs up anger.

14. LIFEJACKETS

One piece of equipment that a responsible boat operator is never without is a lifejacket, or a PFD (personal flotation device). Technically a lifejacket and a PFD are not the same, but they serve much the same purpose. Boating regulations require that there must be at least one lifejacket or PFD for every person on board a boat. They are stowed in a safe, easily accessible location on the sailboat. The captain should inform every passenger and crew of their location. Lifejackets are to keep a person afloat if they are in the water. This equipment is for emergency use. It can save your life.

Even Christians face emergencies. There are times when we are thrown into the deep, when we are over our heads. There are times when we face storms, just as anyone else does—a loved one dies, we face serious health problems, our marriage is in trouble, we lose our job. An old gospel song says, "With Christ in the vessel, we'll smile at the storm." As Christians we have fellowship with Jesus every day, but it is assuring to know that He is particularly near us during life's emergency situations. You can also rely on the support of other Christians to pray with and for you and to see you through.

PSALM 50:15

...call on me in the day of trouble; I will deliver you,

15. LIGHTHOUSES

Lighthouses hold a lot of romance. The picture of a lighthouse standing tall against a darkening sky, shining its light across the billowing waves, inspires and encourages us. The stores of lighthouse keepers and daring rescues hold our imagination. Today most lighthouses are unoccupied; they are simply automated lights fixed to structures on shore. Nevertheless, they still provide navigational aid to sailors at night, leading them to a harbour or warning them about dangers.

Lighthouses remind me of those people in my life who inspire me. They are the strong, stalwart Christians who have held their place amid the storms of doubt and the waves of discouragement. They have proven by their years of steadfastness that they can be trusted, that their advice is sound and that they can be relied upon. As you reflect upon your life think about those people who have inspired you. Thank God for those who continue to shine a light for you, warning you of dangers and directing you to where you should go.

MATTHEW 5:14

"You are the light of the world."

16. Charts

I like to sail on Lake Simcoe, in Southern Ontario. Consisting of approximately 300 square miles of surface area and 144 miles of shoreline, it is big enough to get lost in. The lake is notorious for its sudden storms that spring up without notice. It also has both deep holes and shallow bays.

For this reason, I carry a chart in my boat. This chart gives me detailed information about the depth of the lake, about where the islands and shoals are and where the buoys are. Using the chart, I can plot my course and stay relatively safe.

As a Christian you also have a chart. It is the Bible. It will not predict your future, but it will provide you with essential information that will enable you to steer your life in the right direction. The Bible is indispensable for anyone who intends to live according to God's will. It provides us with God's rules for living. It inspires us with stories of faith. It shows us Jesus.

Ronald Reagan, the 40th president of the United States said: "Within the covers of the Bible are the answers for all the problems men face." Charles Dickens said: "The New Testament is the very best book that ever was or ever will be known in the world."

Read your Bible regularly. Live by its teachings and you will sail on to Heaven's shore

Psalm 119:105

Your word is a lamp for my feet, a light on my path.

17. ANCHOR

Anchors are not as simple as they seem. The traditional *fisherman's anchor* holds well but is very heavy. The *plough* design (which looks like a plough) is hinged and light. The *Bruce* design is a variation of the *plough* but is not hinged. The *Danforth* is hinged and light and can also be stowed flat, which is the one I use. The top quality of an anchor is its holding power. It is important also that the anchor be securely attached to the boat with a chain or a combination of chain and line (rope). If everything is right, your anchor will hold and your boat will be secure.

An old gospel song asks the question:
"Will your anchor hold in the storms of life,
When the clouds unfold their wings of strife?
When the strong tides lift, and the cables strain,
Will your anchor drift or firm remain?"

To answer these questions in the affirmative, we need to know that we are anchored in Christ. He is the rock that will not move. Our faith is our anchor. The grace of God is the anchor line. With our faith strong and our anchor secure, we will be able to face everything that life throws at us.

ROMANS 8:38, 39

For I am convinced that neither death nor life...nor anything else in all creation, will be able to separate us from the love of God that is in Christ Jesus our Lord.

18. Buoys

If you've ever travelled on a boat of any kind you probably have noticed buoys floating in the water. These are navigational aids, usually made of steel and painted in various colours. They are anchored in place to give directions to boats. They serve two main purposes: to give directions or to warn of dangers. The colours and markings give directions so that the captain can know where to steer his boat. It is essential for a boat operator to follow these directions carefully.

In your life there are people who act like buoys. By that I mean they give you advice (sometimes whether you ask for it or not). They sometimes warn you about dangers. They sometimes tell you what you should do (in their opinion). Unlike buoys, which cannot be ignored, the people who give you direction can be ignored. You need to know who is giving the advice and be able to weigh it carefully. We should not dismiss all advice outright. Sometimes the adviser is God-sent. We can learn from others, but we must take all advice carefully.

Proverbs 11:14 (NKJV)

Where there is no counsel, the people fall;
But in the multitude of counselors there is safety.

19. MOTOR

Even on my sailboat I have a motor. It is a 4-stroke, 8-hp Honda. The motor is attached to the transom by means of an adjustable wooden plate so that the motor can be lowered into the water when the boat is not under sail. A rubber gas line runs from the motor to a gas tank. The motor is a backup power source. I have done up to five months of sailing using less than twenty dollars' worth of gasoline. Because I have the motor serviced it is reliable, and I don't have to worry when the wind fails or a storm blows me off course.

In life you depend on certain things for your physical and spiritual well-being. You rely on your employer to provide you with a reasonable income. You depend on your church to provide you with good biblical teaching and inspiring worship. You count on your friends for encouragement. But what happens if one or more of these fail? What is your backup plan? What are your alternatives? God has promised never to fail us, never to leave us. We should never think of God as Plan B. He is Plan A all the time. While other sources of inspiration or support may fail, God never will.

HEBREWS 13:5 (NKJV)

For He Himself has said, "I will never leave you nor forsake you."

20. Crew

The cockpit is the hub of a sailboat. This is the area toward the back of the boat where the crew sit and where most of the work of sailing is done. The cockpit on my boat has benches along each side to accommodate four to six people. Here is where the tiller is located to steer the boat. And all the lines attached to the foresail and the mainsail lead back to the cockpit. Here, too, is where the crew (all passengers are considered crew) usually socialize in comfort and safety.

Even Jesus did not sail alone. He had a crew who worked with him, and sometimes literally sailed with him on the Sea of Galilee. These were Peter, James, John, Andrew and eight others. There were twelve men whom Jesus called Apostles. Jesus was the captain, and they were the crew. Where Jesus went, they went. What Jesus did, they did. They worked together, prayed together, and ate together.

The cockpit reminds me of those places in our Christian life where we meet with other Christians to work and have fellowship. This can be as part of a project team helping with such things as cleaning the church grounds, preparing a church supper, visiting shut-ins or organizing a music concert. It's fun to be part of a crew, to know that you have a job and are counted. Get involved in service with others and you will discover the joy of fellowship in doing.

1 Corinthians 3:9

For we are co-workers in God's service

Questions for Reflection and Discussion

1. If you were a boat, what kind would your be, and why?

2. How do you handle the storms of life?

3. Why does God allow storms to come into our lives?

4. To what extent does God direct your life—is He the Captain or a passenger?

5. How can you live life on an "even keel"?

6. How can a man best navigate through life?

7. Where are your havens of rest, your marinas of support?

PART 4

FISHERMEN

1. Calling

I have been fishing since as long as I can remember. As a child of five or six, I used to catch little fish in a bottle from a creek near our house. Later when our family moved to another town and built a house near a river, I spent many happy days fishing with a rod and line. As an adult I have fished in  many lakes and streams, often accompanied by my wife who also enjoys fishing.

When I read in the Bible how Jesus called His first disciples, I was thrilled to learn that those first followers were fishermen. There were Peter and his brother Andrew, and James and his brother John. They owned a boat and earned their living catching fish from the Sea of Galilee. When Jesus called them He said, "Follow me, and I will make you fishers of men." To be a follower of Jesus is much like being a fisherman. You are being called to help catch people and bring them into the Kingdom of God.

To be a "fisher of men" is the calling of all Christians. This work is not just for the pastor or the evangelist; it is for everyone. Some are called to bring in big catches. Others are called to bring in key catches. But all are called to fish.

MATTHEW 4:19 (KJV)

And he saith unto them, Follow me, and I will make you fishers of men.

2. LOVE

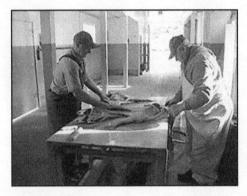

There are fishermen and then there are fishermen. They are not all alike. Two big categories are commercial fishermen and recreational fishermen. I belong to the latter group because I don't earn my living from fishing. However, I still take my fishing seriously. Among the recreational fishermen there are the deep-sea fishermen who go after the big fish such as sailfish and swordfish, and there are those who prefer to fish in streams and lakes and bring home pan fish for a good old-fashioned fish fry. There are fishermen who prefer to use bait and those who prefer to fly fish. All fishermen have one thing in common: they love what they do.

What can be said of fishermen can also be said of Christians. We are not all alike. Two big categories are Catholic and Protestant. Then there are sub-categories such as Evangelical, Holiness, and Charismatic, to name just a few. Some Christians like to worship with loud, contemporary music, some with brass bands and orchestras and some with soft organ music. There are Christians who prefer to worship with large crowds of thousands, and others who prefer to belong to a small congregation of a hundred or less. But all real Christians have two things in common: they love Jesus and want to follow Him, and they love their brothers and sisters in the Lord.

JOHN 13:35

"By this everyone will know that you are my disciples, if you love one another."

3. Species

According to researchers there are tens of thousands (some say up to 40,000) species of fish in the world. These range in size from the huge whale shark to tiny krill. Some fish, like the great white shark, are notorious for their ferocity. Some, such as the scorpion fish, are venomous. There are fish that produce electricity and fish that change colour. There are fish that are covered with thorns and fish that look like jelly. There are fish that are good for food and fish that are delightful to look at. And all kinds of them show up in a fishing net.

Jesus once compared the Kingdom of Heaven to a net that was cast into the sea (Matthew 13:47–50) and which caught many species of fish. The good fish were kept, but the bad fish were thrown away. As with fish, so with people—there are many different kinds of them. Some people are like sharks, vicious and cruel. Some are like jellyfish with no backbone. Some are like clams who just sit still and neither do nor say anything. Some are beautiful. All kinds of people will show up in our churches. If you were to compare yourself to a fish, what kind of fish would you be?

Matthew 13:47 (KJV)

Again, the kingdom of heaven is like unto a net, that was cast into the sea, and gathered of every kind

4. Methods

When I was a boy my father tried to teach me to knit a net. Growing up in a small fishing village around boats and wharfs, he knew a thing or two about fishing. I actually learned how to use a fishnet needle to create several rows of mesh. However, since netting was not my favourite method to fish, I learned more practical skills like how to cast a lure and bait with my casting rod to catch trout and how to use my fly rod for salmon. The point is that there are different ways to catch fish. No one particular way is better than another. The angler doesn't judge the spin caster. And the seiner doesn't despise the long-liner.

Different Christians go about witnessing for Jesus in different ways. Some, like the great evangelists, speak to thousands in stadiums and arenas. Some Christians proclaim their faith by wearing T-shirts with Christian slogans or by putting Christian messages on bumper stickers. Some even tattoo their witness on their flesh. Other Christians quietly go about their lives and let their actions be their witness, responding to those who inquire as to why they are different. No matter how we witness, our goal is the same—to be "fishers of men (and women)" for Christ. Let us not judge one another's methods, but rejoice over each soul won.

Mark 9:38–40

"Teacher," said John, "we saw someone driving out demons in your name and we told him to stop, because he was not one of us."

"Do not stop him," Jesus said. "For no one who does a miracle in my name can in the next moment say anything bad about me, for whoever is not against us is for us.

5. Opportunity

A vid fishermen will fish any-where they can legally get a line in the water. I've fished in British Columbia, amid the tower-ing Rocky Mountains. I've fished on the Great Lakes. I have fished in the ponds of the East Coast, far back behind the marshes and deep within the forest. And I've fished in great salmon rivers and in little streams that flowed through culverts under-neath highways. Sometimes, in the most unlikely of places, I have pulled out a large trout to my own astonishment.

As Christians we should not limit our "fishing" (that is, witnessing) to those places we are familiar with or where we feel we have a good chance to succeed. Sometimes we can influence someone for Christ in the most unusual places and in the most unlikely circumstances. Jesus said that His followers will witness for him "in the uttermost parts of the earth." That includes the most unlikely places such as the factory, the golf course, the shopping centre and right in our own backyard. You don't have to wait for the perfect place to fish. Let your light shine just where you are.

Acts 1:8

But you will receive power when the Holy Spirit comes on you; and you will be my witnesses in Jerusalem, and in all Judea and Samaria, and to the ends of the earth."

6. COST

Fishing can be very expensive. There are people who invest thousands of dollars in boats, motors, boat trailers, downriggers, hip waders, rods, reels, lines, lures and tackle boxes. Some spend thousands more for the privilege of flying to remote areas and paying a guide. But there are also a lot of people who, with a modest investment of less than a hundred dollars, enjoy sitting on a wharf or strolling along the banks of a stream and casting in a hook and worm. Purchase good equipment, but don't go overboard. The excitement is found in using your knowledge and skill to catch a fish. Sherlock Holmes would say it's the "thrill of the chase." This can be experienced regardless of the kind of equipment used.

When witnessing for Jesus you might be tempted to think that you need expensive "equipment." You might think you need to take special training, enrol in an expensive public relations course or go to Bible school. To be an evangelist you don't need a TV program, or an arena, or even a congregation. Any Christian can be a witness for Jesus, and any Christian can be an evangelist in their own right. The first disciples were "fishers of men" not because they had big budgets for an outreach program, but simply because they let their light shine and took every opportunity to speak boldly for their Lord. All of us can experience the thrill of the chase as we pursue people for Christ.

ACTS 3:6

Then Peter said, "Silver or gold I do not have, but what I do have I give you. In the name of Jesus Christ of Nazareth, walk."

7. LURES

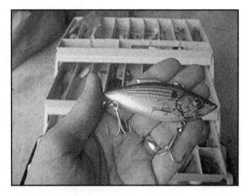

Most recreational fisher-men, including myself, have a large variety of lures in their tackle boxes. These range from simple spinners to complex lures with sound and lights. In the fishing supply aisle of our local hardware store, I often inspect the latest lures when I am there. Lures have one object—to attract fish. They do this by resembling prey. The lure, through movement, vibration and colour, attracts the fish's attention. If one lure does not work, then I try another and another, until I finally find one that works in the particular place where I am fishing.

As Christians we should be living lives that attract others to Christ. Our life-style, our morals, our beliefs, our behaviour and speech should be like a fishing lure—they should attract the attention of unbelievers in a positive way. The early Salvation Army was very good at attracting people to the gospel. They did this first by their uniforms and music, but even more so by their good deeds and caring ministry. People outside the church saw the positive changes in their friends who were converted, and this attracted them to learn more about the gospel. Strive to be an "alluring" Christian.

1 TIMOTHY 4:12

...set an example for the believers in speech, in conduct, in love, in faith and in purity.

8. BAIT

The big difference between lures and bait (besides the fact that lures are artificial and bait is natural) is that lures are long lasting but bait is temporary. Once I purchase a lure and add it to my collection, it is always available to me. It is a permanent part of my fishing gear. With bait, such as worms, minnows or leeches, I have to get a fresh supply almost every time I go fishing. (I have been known, however, to keep leftover worms in the refrigerator for a few days until my next trip.) But both lures and bait have the same purpose—to attract fish.

Staying on the topic of Christian witness, lures can be compared to those aspects of our Christian life that are always a part of us—our character, our beliefs and our lifestyle. Bait can be compared to those things that are seasonal or serendipitous. Inviting an unbelieving friend to your home for a barbeque can be bait. It will put a good taste in his mouth, not only for the meat but for your thoughtfulness. Helping someone in trouble can be bait, because it allows them to taste the fruit of the Spirit that is growing in your life. Every contact you have with others will give them a chance to taste the goodness of God through you. And remember to keep your bait fresh.

PSALM 34:8

Taste and see that the Lord is good,
blessed is the one who takes refuge in him.

9. LINE

B esides a rod, lures and bait, recreational fishermen also need fishing line. For those using spin cast rods, the line used is usually monofilament, made of a single strand of clear nylon or polyethylene. Anglers who fish with artificial flies use lines that are coated with a buoyant material to allow them to float. Lines are usually designed to be as unnoticeable as possible to the fish. Otherwise  the fish may be scared off and not approach the bait. The line also has to be strong to be able to hold the fish and bring it in.

Jesus wants us to catch people for the Kingdom of God so that they can have life. We lure them with our genuine faith and moral lifestyle. We bait them with our kindness and friendliness. But we draw them into the Kingdom with chords of love. Our motive must always be love and our methods must always be kind and genuine. We must also be gentle in our approach, almost invisible, like the fishing line, but also strong in our faith so that we don't lose the souls we are trying to win. Some Christians, by being over-aggressive in their witness, have scared off unbelievers. A gentle approach will allow you to get closer to those who may be suspicious or cynical of religion.

COLOSSIANS 3:12

Therefore, as God's chosen people, holy and dearly loved, clothe yourselves with compassion, kindness, humility, gentleness and patience.

10. OFFSHORE

If you've ever watched the movie *Jaws*, you may recall the famous line uttered by Sheriff Brody to Captain Quint when they saw the size of the shark circling their small boat: "You're gonna need a bigger boat." I've never been in the situation where I needed a bigger boat because of the size of the fish I had on my line. However, there have been times when I wished I had a bigger boat because of the size of the waves and the strength of the wind. Generally speaking, a bigger boat means three things: it's safer, you can go offshore farther and you can take more people with you. I have fished from a canoe (not recommended) and fished from a 20-foot boat with a group of friends (much more fun).

In your Christian life you can try to "go it alone," but it is safer and more fun to go with friends. And I believe that you will go farther in your faith when you have friends who will journey with you. If our life can be compared to a fishing boat (remember, we are "fishers of men"), then some of us have boats that are too small. We are timid and hug the shore. We go after the small fry when we could be hunting tuna. An old gospel song says, "Launch out into the deep and let the shore lines go." That's what we need to do if we want to catch the trophies for the Lord.

MARK 16:15

He said to them, "Go into all the world and preach the gospel to all creation.

11. PATIENCE

T he first disciples of Jesus were
fishermen. I think He chose
them after observing them at work.
Fishermen need to possess specific
qualities of character to be successful.
These qualities easily transfer to the
work of evangelism. Take, for example, patience. I'm not a patient man by
nature. I get frustrated easily, which
tends to make me upset and even quit

what I'm doing when things don't go my way. However, when it comes to fishing
I have been known to fish for hours on end without catching a single fish. I have
felt a fish nibble on my line and watched it swim by, and I've waited and waited,
patiently enticing it until finally it grabbed on and I landed a prize catch.

Witnessing for Jesus often requires a similar kind of patience. We may be
impatient by nature, but God can help us to take things easy when we are sharing
our faith. People may come into our lives who are curious about Christianity. They
are not eager about it. They are not going to grab on to our lifestyle, but they show
a little interest. They may want to know what goes on at church, what the Bible is
about and who Jesus is. Witnessing to such people requires great patience. Take
things at their pace, not yours. You may go years without success, but a true fisherman does not give up easily. Many a potential convert has been scared off by an
over-eager Christian who did not have the patience to wait. In your witnessing, be
patient with the unbeliever who has come into your sphere of influence.

2 Peter 3:9

The Lord is not slow in keeping his promise, as some understand slowness.
Instead he is patient with you, not wanting anyone to perish, but everyone
to come to repentance.

12. PERSISTENCE

 Y ou are no doubt familiar with the old adage "If at first you don't succeed, try, try again." That facet of your character that enables you to keep trying after you have failed is called persistence. Fishermen do not catch fish every time they throw a hook into the water. I enjoy fly fishing. This kind of angling involves casting the fly across the water over and over again, often hundreds of times without a strike. I often have to change the kind of fly I use. After one fly fails to entice a fish, I take it off and try one of a different colour or a different shape. I may go through a dozen flies before finding the one that works. This is persistence.

In our Christian life and service, we will not be successful at everything we do every time we do it. We will sometimes meet with failure. But like a fly fisherman, you need to keep trying and to try different things. Take, for example, your private prayer time. You may try praying early in the morning but find that you are not a morning person. Don't give up; try an evening time or even a noon talk with God. Perhaps you are looking for an avenue in which to serve. You try the choir, but find you can't sing. You try children's work, but can't communicate well with children. Don't give up; try something else until you find what works for you. This is persistence.

MATTHEW 7:7

Ask and it will be given to you; seek and you will find; knock and the door will be opened to you.

13. FAITH

Fishermen are people of faith. Faith by definition is belief and trust in something without absolute scientific proof. When I fish I have to have faith or I would not venture near the water. I have faith that the line I'm using will not break, that my boat will not sink and that there are fish out there even though I can't see them. I have faith that if I keep fishing long enough and try hard enough I will catch a fish, even though some days this seems unlikely. I envision fish in my frying pan and I have faith enough to believe that that vision will come true.

Everyone has faith. Even those who claim to be atheists have faith. We get aboard an airplane and believe that the pilot is skilled and sane, even though we've never met them. We have faith in the mechanics, electricians and machinists who built and maintain the aircraft, even though we don't know them and don't know how everything works on a plane. When we buy groceries we put our faith in the produces, manufacturers and distributors to provide us with healthy food. Faith is not illogical. It is necessary for life. How much more is it necessary for death? Faith in Jesus takes away fear. Faith in Jesus will enable us to live holy lives. Putting our trust in Him will bring us to Heaven.

JOHN 14:1

(Jesus said) *"Do not let your hearts be troubled. You believe in God; believe also in me."*

14. COURAGE

I f you've ever seen the movie *The Perfect Storm* or watched the TV series *Deadliest Catch*, you are aware of how dangerous commercial fishing is. (My most dangerous catch is usually ice fishing—trying to keep my fingers and toes from freezing.) As a recreational fisherman, I have to take my hat off to those men and women who travel hundreds of miles from land to make a living from the sea. In the days of sailing ships, before much of today's safety gear and rescue techniques were developed, fishing was far more dangerous than it is today. The highest number of widows per capita were in small fishing villages because of the many men lost at sea. Even today, it takes a lot of courage to be a commercial fisherman.

For most of us in North America, living a Christian life is about as dangerous as recreational fishing. We have to have the interest and the patience and the persistence and the faith, but it doesn't take a lot of courage. The most opposition we face is verbal—someone disagrees with us or perhaps laughs at our beliefs. Our biggest fear is being ridiculed or rejected. In some countries Christians need a lot more courage. When they speak up for Jesus there is a real possibility they could be jailed or beaten or killed. Some Christians have lost their homes and property. Some have lost their families. Many Christians are tortured, even today, for their faith. Let us use the freedom of religion that we have and let us continue to support and pray for those Christians who face death for Jesus.

REVELATION 2:10

Do not be afraid of what you are about to suffer. I tell you, the devil will put some of you in prison to test you, and you will suffer persecution for ten days. Be faithful, even to the point of death, and I will give you life as your victor's crown.

15. KNOWLEDGE

There is a lot more to fishing than simply throwing a hook and line in the water. There are many things to learn in order to become successful at the sport. A beginner needs to learn such basic things as how to load a line on a reel, how to operate the reel, how to tie a hook, lure and fly on a line, how to cast the line, how to retrieve the line, how to set the hook and how to land a fish. After that there is such knowledge as knowing where to fish, knowing what lure, bait or fly to use in a particular place, knowing the best times to fish. And on and on we can go with things to learn in order to become an expert fisherman.

When Jesus called His disciples He said, "Follow me, and I will make you fishers of men." They knew a lot about fishing for fish, but they did not know a lot about fishing for souls. This was something that they would have to learn. Jesus would make them fishers of men. This was knowledge they would have to acquire. For the following three years they were apprentices in Jesus' class. He taught them knowledge and skills to become soul-winners. They learned both theology and practice. Under His tutelage they became evangelists and eventually went on to win the world for Jesus.

JOHN 6:45

(Jesus said) *It is written in the Prophets: 'They will all be taught by God.' Everyone who has heard the Father and learned from him comes to me.*

16. Enjoyment

The joy of fishing can only be known by those who fish. Reading about fishing will not impart to you the joy of fishing. Watching fishing shows on television will not give you the joy of fishing. Listening to fishermen tell and retell their fishing stories will not convey the joy of fishing. You cannot experience the joy of fishing until you actually fish. You have to spend time on or near the water. You have to smell the fresh air, the forest and the meadow. You have to sense your boat bobbing in the waves. You have to feel the tug of a fish on your line. You have to play a fish and win to know the joy of the experience.

The joy of the Lord can only be known by those who know the Lord. You can study the Christian religion. You can read the Bible. You can go to church and Sunday school. You can participate in the rituals. But until you experience for yourself the Presence of Jesus in your life, you will not know the joy He gives. The joy of Christianity can only be known by those who know Christ. You have to spend time with Him. You have to sense Him near you. You have to feel the tug of His Spirit on your heart. Only then will you experience the joy of the Lord for yourself.

JOHN 15:11

I have told you this so that my joy may be in you and that your joy may be complete.

17. Fishing Trip

A h, the good, old fishing trip. I've had many of these over the years, some with an old friend, some with a group of friends and some with my wife, who by the way also loves fishing. After one of the men makes a suggestion of going fishing, the fun begins. It is usually a few days or weeks before-

hand. We decide where to go, when to go, how to get there, who will come with us, what to bring and what to eat. When the day comes we eagerly set out, usually around sunup. We may bring a boat or fish from shore. We have lunch, around a campfire if possible. And we may catch some fish. But the big bonus is the fellowship and the strengthening of bonds between like-minded persons.

In the Church this fellowship and bonding often happen around a project that the church members undertake together. While Sunday worship is spiritually beneficial, and Bible studies build up our faith, nothing quite matches the experience of a group of like-minded believers working together to accomplish something for the Kingdom. I remember working with a group of men from the church, cutting trees and bringing firewood to a man who was disabled. I recall working with men renovating a church—the sound of hammers and saws and good-natured teasing being more inspiring than some sermons. Perhaps now is the time for you to call some of your Christian friends and plan such a project. You'll be blessed as you bless others.

1 John 3:18 (NKJV)

My little children, let us not love in word or in tongue, but in deed and in truth.

18. Bonding

There is a bond among fishermen that allows them to instantly relate to each other even though on many other levels they may be total strangers. Two men can be sitting at a table awkwardly wondering what they have in common and struggling to find something to talk about. If one happens to mention fishing and the other is also a fisherman, then they are off and running. Each will try to outdo the other with fishing tales, and the fish will grow bigger with each telling. They will talk about favourite places to fish, about memorable catches and about the one that got away. Each will instantly understand the other, and their fellowship will be real.

The fellowship of Christians is like that and more so. When travelling on vacation I meet total strangers. Often we have little in common, but if we find out that we are both Christians, then instantly we have a bond that is beyond all others. We realize that no longer are we strangers. We are more than friends. We are brothers and sisters in Christ. Our theology may be slightly different. Our worship may not be exactly the same. But at heart we both love the Lord and recognize each other as part of His family. We can talk about our faith and share with each other how God works that out in our lives. How wonderful it is to belong to the fellowship of believers.

Acts 2:44

All the believers were together and had everything in common.

19. Seasons

Fishing has its seasons. Different species of fish may be legally caught at different times of the year. As a boy growing up on the East Coast, I could hardly wait for the summer trout season to begin. It lasted from the middle of June to the middle of September, which coincided nicely with the summer holidays. When I

grew older I got interested in salmon fishing and enjoyed catching those in their season. When I lived in Ontario, I looked forward to bass season. Some species, like perch, can be caught all year round. Commercial fishermen also go after different species in different seasons. I remember helping my father catch squid in their season and helping a friend haul his lobster traps in their season.

The Bible says, "There is a time for everything, and a season for every activity under the heavens" (Ecclesiastes 3:1). This verse, in fact the entire chapter, was made famous by the Byrds in their 1965 hit *Turn, Turn, Turn*. It talks about the seasons of life. Just as there are different seasons for fishing, there are different times in our life for doing particular things. Whether witnessing (there is "a time to be silent and a time to speak") or ministering ("a time to plant") or serving ("a time to love"), everything has its season. But some activities, like perch fishing, have no season. They can and should be done all year round. Living our faith is one of those activities.

1 Peter 3:15

Always be prepared to give an answer to everyone who asks you to give the reason for the hope that you have. But do this with gentleness and respect,

20. Rewards

Fishing is a rewarding experience. The challenge of outwitting a fish in its natural environment is thrilling. The skill of landing a large fish using a tiny, barbless fly hook attached to an 8-pound test line with a rod that is bending like the letter U is exhilarating. And the smell of fresh fish in the frying pan (as well as the taste of the delicious meal) is heavenly. Of course there are many other rewards, too: the fresh air and sunshine on your face, the sound of loons on the lake, the sight of mountains, streams and forest, the fellowship of other fishermen and sometimes the solitude of sitting by oneself and feeling close to the Creator.

But nothing is as rewarding as the Christian life. Jesus talked about it in terms of joy. He described it as abundant life. To know that your life has meaning and that it will go on forever is the greatest thrill there is. To know Christ as your Saviour and friend is the greatest knowledge there is. To relate to God as His child—His son or daughter—to call Him Father and to know that He loves you more than you can imagine, is the greatest relationship there is. Yes, following Christ sometimes has its difficulties, but these are only like fishing on a rainy day or casting your line into the wind compared to the great and wonderful rewards for the true follower.

JOHN 10:10

I have come that they may have life, and have it to the full.

Questions for Reflection and Discussion

1. To what extent do you consider yourself a "fisher of men"?

2. What are some ways men can attract other men to Christ?

3. What would scare men from committing their life to Christ?

4. What gifts or qualifications does a "fisher of men" need?

5. How important are patience and persistence when witnessing?

6. How can a man improve his fishing (witnessing) skills?

7. Is the calling to be a "fisher of men" for everyone or only a chosen few? Explain.

PART 5

CARS

1. LICENCE

Growing up in a small town back east, I was more than a little envious at some of my classmates whose families were rich enough to buy them cars. My last year of high school was 1964–65, the same year that the Ford Mustang was released. And one of my classmates drove one to school. I did not have a driver's licence but I was permitted to drive my father's 1954 GMC pickup truck, mostly when he was aboard. Sometimes I took it and drove around the back roads with my best friend, never thinking about insurance or the consequences of getting stopped by the police. I remember crashing through a fence and driving into a clump of alders. My father said I could get my licence when I could afford to buy my own vehicle, which took another five years.

Starting out on the Christian life is much like learning to drive. It is exciting. It is thrilling. It is new. For a person who has never been saved to suddenly come to know the Lord as their Saviour and Friend, the experience is like being born again. A whole new world opens up to them. Like a new driver, they have freedom they never knew before. They are free from the old lifestyle of drugs, alcohol and immorality. They are free to forgive others. They have the power to let go of old resentments and old habits. They have a licence to love.

JOHN 1:12 (KJV)

But as many as received him, to them gave he power to become the sons of God, even to them that believe on his name:

2. CHOICE

Do you remember your first car? Who can forget? After my first year at university, I accepted a teaching position. The pay was low in those days—two hundred dollars a month. I could not afford to buy a car, so I bought a motorcycle. It wasn't until three years later when my fiancée and I pooled our financial resources that I (we) got our first car. It was a 1969 Vauxhall Viva, which we bought in 1970. It was a small two-door car with a four-cylinder motor and an automatic transmission. We paid about $1,200 for it. It was what some of my friends called a "gutless wonder." We barely made it up the mountains of the Cabot Trail on our honeymoon. But it was great going downhill!

Our choice of car was limited by our budget and what was available. But choosing a car is not the most important choice of your life. There are many, more important choices. Choosing who to marry, for example, is much more important. Choosing your career is much more important. Choosing whether or not to have children is much more important. There are dozens of choices more important than which car to purchase. But all life's choices have consequences. It is therefore important to make those choices carefully and prayerfully. If we choose God first and then ask Him to help us with all our other choices, then tomorrow will not be so scary.

PSALM 25:12

Who, then, are those who fear the Lord?
He will instruct them in the ways they should choose.

3. VALUE

O ver the years that I have been driving, I have owned eleven vehicles—eight cars and three mini-vans. Of these, five were bought new, five came off a used car lot and one I bought from a friend. When purchasing a

vehicle one question that has to be answered early in the process is whether to buy new or used. My father used to say, "Don't buy someone else's junk." His opinion was forged from his experiences with a few lemons he purchased used over the years. While his advice is still valid, I have learned to appreciate the fact that there is value in both new and used cars. Conversely, "junk" can come in new packaging as well as old.

In our Christian life we should not be too hasty to label anything as "junk." I have known Christians to dismiss old hymns and traditional worship services as being broken down and ineffective. I have also known Christians to label contemporary worship songs as being all show and no substance. The truth is that there are some old hymns that should be thrown out and there are some new songs that should never be sung. On the other hand, there are some old songs and old traditions that carry a lot of meaning and should be treasured. Likewise, there are some beautiful new worship songs that need to be learned and adopted. What holds true for worship songs also holds true for people. It's not age but quality that counts.

MATTHEW 13:52

He said to them, "Therefore every teacher of the law who has become a disciple in the kingdom of heaven is like the owner of a house who brings out of his storeroom new treasures as well as old."

4. Cost

Cars are expensive. Even those you may buy at a bargain. Besides the price of the car itself, there are many other expenditures to consider when calculating the true cost of ownership. If you have to get a loan, there is the interest to be paid. Then there is the annual insurance cost. After that there are the maintenance costs—oil changes, replacing worn tires, breaks and burnt-out headlights. Then there is the cost of gasoline. And inevitably there will be the cost of repairs as the body begins to rust, the engine begins to lose power and nicks and dents appear from occasional bumps with guard rails, fence posts and other cars in parking lots. So when buying a car, count the real cost.

The same is true in life. Everything costs. But not everything has value. We need to calculate the true cost of the decisions we make. For example, someone may say, "I can't go to university because it costs too much." Education is costly, but what are the costs of not having an education? Its true value is beyond calculation. The same can be said of many other things—marriage, children, career and friendships. Likewise, the decision of whether or not to follow Christ should be considered carefully. It will cost you a lot to be a true follower, but it will cost you infinitely more to reject Him.

Matthew 16:26 (NKJV)

For what profit is it to a man if he gains the whole world, and loses his own soul?

5. BRAND

B rand loyalty is a big thing in the car industry. My dad purchased his 1954 GMC pickup in 1955. He kept it for ten years. For a while we called it Chevy, then as it became part of the family we called it Betsy. It was the only vehicle I knew during my growing-up years. We loved that old Chev, but we weren't hardcore loyals; we were switchers, driven by what we could afford. So over the years I have owned Chevs, Fords, AMC cars and Dodges. With the exception of my first car, the Viva, I have stuck with North American brands. So I suppose there is some loyalty there to the domestic vehicles.

Loyalty is also important in our faith, much more important than loyalty to car manufacturers. The Bible word for loyalty is "faithfulness." It used to be that Christians counted loyalty to their church as something very important. If they were born into a particular denomination, they stayed as such until they died. Today, loyalty to a particular denomination is not so important in most people's minds. This results in what some call "church hopping." While "switching brands" is sometimes necessary, it should not be a regular habit. There is something to be said about putting down roots and becoming a faithful member of your church. But in the end the brand loyalty that really matters is faithfulness to Christ.

MATTHEW 25:21

"His master replied, 'Well done, good and faithful servant! You have been faithful with a few things; I will put you in charge of many things. Come and share your master's happiness!'

6. MOTOR

Every guy who goes looking for a vehicle wants to look under the hood. He wants to see if the motor looks clean or if it is covered with oil. But more importantly, he wants to know how big it is. How many cylinders are there? What is the cubic inch measurement of the engine? What is the horsepower? Even if he can't afford to drive a muscle care with a 350 engine, he still likes to dream. He may settle for a four-cylinder hybrid that sips gasoline like a tea connoisseur at a taste test. In the end the choice is made between power and miles per gallon. In reality, engine size doesn't matter; it's what you do with it that counts.

In life we all like to dream big. We all would like to accomplish some big thing and leave a big footprint behind us on the world's stage. Some have done that—Martin Luther, Winston Churchill, Abraham Lincoln, Billy Graham, to name a few. But most of us play minor parts on the stage of life. Or do we? What may appear to the world to be a minor part may be a critical part of God's great plan. Think for a moment of Martin Luther's teacher and Abraham Lincoln's mother, and the person who led Billy Graham to faith in Christ. You probably don't know their names, yet the parts they played in the lives of others were invaluable. In the service of the Lord, the size of our ministry does not matter. Doing God's will is all that counts.

JOHN 3:30 (KJV)

He must increase, but I must decrease.

7. Sparkplugs

Imbedded in a car's gasoline engine are small porcelain and metal devices called spark plugs. Your car may have four, six or eight, depending on the size of your engine. One end of each plug reaches into the engine's cylinders. The other end protrudes from the side or top of the engine and is connected by a wire to the car's electrical system. When current flows, a spark ignites the gasoline in the cylinder chamber. In my younger days, when engines were much simpler, I would regularly replace these plugs myself. It was a fun thing to do in my driveway on a warm Saturday morning. There is something to be said of a guy buried to his waist under the hood of his car, doing his own maintenance.

An old camp song begins, "It only takes a spark to get a fire going." Likewise, without that spark the car is going nowhere. The same is true of any Christian endeavour. Nothing will get done for the Lord unless someone is willing to be the spark that gets the fire going. How often have you heard it said (or perhaps you've said it yourself) "Someone should do something about that"? Perhaps it was a Sunday school class that had no teacher, or homeless people who needed shelter, or unsaved people who needed to hear the gospel. Can you think of yourself as being a "spark plug" for Jesus?

Psalm 104:4 (NKJV)

Who makes His angels spirits, His ministers a flame of fire.

8. Filters

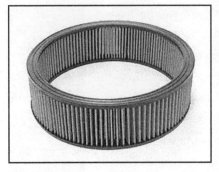

Your car is equipped with a number of filters—air filter, oil filter, gas filter. Some cars also have a filter for the air conditioning unit. Filters by definition clean dirt from contaminating the thing they are filtering. The air filter insures that clean air enters the cylinders. The oil filter keeps the oil clean. The gas filter catches any contaminants that are in the gas. And the air conditioning filter makes sure that passengers and driver breathe fresh, clean air. I used to change the air filter and oil filter myself, but now I leave it to the kids at the quick oil change garage.

The world around us is filled with things that can contaminate your life. Things like pornography, drugs, alcohol and coarse language. Television, movies and the Internet all carry their share of contaminants. As Christians we need to filter out of our lives all those things that soil our witness and make us unclean in our hearts and minds. The filter that we use is the Bible. The word of God and the teachings of Jesus are our standard. By applying this filter to everything we encounter, we can determine whether they are clean or dirty.

Psalm 119:9

How can a young person stay on the path of purity?
By living according to your word.

9. OIL

Every mechanic will tell you that oil is the lifeblood of your car's engine. According to carbibles.com (gotta love that name), engine oil "stops all the metal surfaces in your engine from grinding together and tearing themselves apart from friction..." It also transfers heat from the engine chamber and keeps all the nasty by-products of com-

bustion in suspension. So there you have it—everything you need to know about engine oil. One more thing—change the oil regularly according to your car's driver's manual.

In the Bible the Church is compared to a human body with many parts, with each individual Christian being a part of the Body of Christ. The Church can just as easily be compared to a car with its many moving parts. Just as in a car engine where metal surfaces can "tear themselves apart from friction," so Church members can "tear each other apart" with infighting, competition and disputes. The oil that keeps the Church running smoothly is the influence of the Holy Spirit uniting us in a bond of love. When things begin to heat up in your church because of friction between members, ask God to anoint you again with the oil of the Spirit so that things will run smoothly.

ROMANS 12:4-5

For just as each of us has one body with many members...so in Christ we, though many, form one body, and each member belongs to all the others.

10. Coolant

Things can get pretty hot under the hood of your car. To keep things cool, your car has a cooling system consisting of a radiator, a thermostat, coolant (usually some kind of antifreeze) and a pump. In the old days of my dad's 1954 Chev pickup, the coolant was plain water and the system did not work really well. I remember us stopping at roadside streams many times to put water in the radiator. And when the engine got hot, so did my dad. It was a challenge for both him and the truck to keep their cool.

It is always important for us as Christians to keep our cool. "Cool, calm and collected," as the old saying goes, is the way we should respond under pressure. But we are not all alike. Some of us have short fuses and tend to lose our cool. Like my dad's old truck, some of us tend to get hot under strain. When that happens we need to have in place a cooling system. Besides taking deep breaths, counting to ten and going for a short walk, we should say a little prayer, ask God to give us His peace and put into His hands whatever it is that is causing us to boil over.

John 14:27

Peace I leave with you; my peace I give you... Do not let your hearts be troubled...

11. Colour

O ver the years, I've learned a few things about paint. The first lesson was that looks can be deceiving. My dad's old '54 truck was originally blue, but there was someone else in town with the same kind of truck that was the same colour. The other driver was on the seedier side of  the law and unfortunately my dad's truck was sometimes mistaken for the other one, and we often had the police on our tail—occasionally following us right to our door. When my parents stepped out of the truck, the police were all apologetic. My dad got fed up with these reoccurrences, so one day he handed me a paintbrush and the two of us set to work hand-painting his truck black. It was not the fanciest paint job but it solved the problem. The truck remained black for the remainder of its years and painting it became an annual spring ritual for us.

As Christians we need to live distinctive lives. It's important that people are able to identify us for who and what we are. It's not good enough for us to simply blend in and be like everyone else. And it's far worse if we are considered not to be Christians at all. The only way that people around us can know us is by our words and actions— "they'll know we are Christians by our love." As a child in Sunday school, I was taught: "Don't be afraid to let your colours show." This was not about the clothes we wore but about lifestyle and faith. Stand up for Jesus. Stand out in the crowd.

1 Peter 2:9 (NKJV)

But you are a chosen generation, a royal priesthood, a holy nation, His own special people, that you may proclaim the praises of Him who called you out of darkness into His marvelous light;

12. Tires

L et's talk about tires. Right now I am driving on four comfortable Michelins. They replaced the original tires that came with my vehicle, which were getting quite worn. When I put the new tires on it was like walking in a new pair of slippers. The ride was smooth and quiet.

Over the years, I have not always been so careful. I have been known to drive on what my friends called "baloney skins"—tires that were tread-less and that had wire showing through the sides. After numerous flat tires and skids into snow banks, I have learned the importance of having good rubber underneath me.

You have no doubt heard the expression "where the rubber meets the road." That phrase refers to the most important point in a situation. This is the point where all our preparation and theory turn into action. We can have a fancy-looking car with a big motor, but if it doesn't have good tires it's not going far. In life we can dress in the finest clothes, study at the best universities, attend the most popular church, but if we don't put our faith into action we are going nowhere. In your Christian life, where does the rubber meet the road? At what point does your faith turn into action?

James 2:17

In the same way, faith by itself, if it is not accompanied by action, is dead.

13. BRAKES

When looking for a new car we ask about the motor, the horsepower, the speed, the comfort of the ride, the handling and all things associated with driving. We take for granted that the car has stopping power. You have only to lose your brakes once to never take them for granted again. I recall losing mine while my wife and I were driving to my parents' house one Christmas. About five miles  from their home the brakes gave out. It was night and late. We slowly crept the rest of the way. My dad had left the garage door open for us and we coasted to a stop by bumping into the back wall. This is not recommended.

Life is fast-paced. We rush from one activity to the next, often boasting about how busy we are. Most of us hate to be idle, hate to have to stop. But there are times when we need to slow down. In fact, there are times when we should slam on the brakes. When we don't have time for our family we need to slow down. When our work is interfering with our health we need to slow down. And when temptations are drawing us into sin we need to slam on the brakes and come to a full stop.

1 CORINTHIANS 15:34

Come back to your senses as you ought, and stop sinning...

14. Lights

It's been said that we don't appreciate something until it's gone. Take signal lights on your car, for example. Last week my left-turn signal light on the front of my car gave out. When making a turn, I had to stick my arm out the window and use hand signals for the few hours before I could replace it. (This was a do-it-yourself job with a bulb from the local auto supply store.) Turn signal lights, headlights, tail lights, break lights, park lights and back-up lights are there for two purposes: to see and to be seen. The headlights enable us to see where we are going at night. The other lights are for people to see us. Both are important.

The Bible talks about spiritual light in the same two ways. God's Spirit and God's word are like the two headlights on our car, showing us the way to go. Our own lifestyle, our words, our actions, our attitudes and our character are like the other lights on the car, showing those around us who we are and what we are doing. We must live by the light God gives us, and we must also let our light shine as a witness for Jesus to those around us.

1 John 1:7

But if we walk in the light, as he is in the light, we have fellowship with one another, and the blood of Jesus, his Son, purifies us from all sin.

15. WINDSHIELD

On a number of occasions, I have been driving and thought that my windshield was clean. Then I found myself driving directly into the sun and, wow, all the dust and grime revealed itself. I could hardly see out the window. Driving in the shade or with the sun behind me was no problem. As soon as the light hit the window, all was revealed. The sad thing was that the dust was on the inside. Keeping the windows clean on the outside was not such a problem, my wipers, along with the rain and an occasional car wash, took care of that. It was the dirt on the inside that was the problem. I had to get out the Windex.

In our Christian life we can often get away with keeping clean on the outside. An occasional visit to church, a few charitable donations, a little volunteer work and we appear to those around us to be upright citizens. But in the light of God's word and in the glow of God's Spirit moving in our hearts, we see what we are on the inside. Jesus had a word for people who appeared clean on the outside but were dirty on the inside. He called them hypocrites. Strive to be pure through and through. Keep the windows to your soul clean.

MATTHEW 23:26

First clean the inside of the cup and dish, and then the outside also will be clean.

16. DASHBOARD

The dashboard of your car is the source of all kinds of vital information necessary for the safe performance of your vehicle. The early cars gave the barest essentials: gas gauge, engine temperature, voltage, odometer, speedometer and high-beam indicator. With electronic dashboards of today we have all that and more. My minivan shows me the oil life, the average amount of fuel consumed per kilometre, that a seatbelt is not fastened and that a door is ajar. It even has a built in satellite system that enables me to phone hands free.

If our lives can be compared to a car, the question we need to consider is, where are we getting the information necessary for a healthy, fulfilling life? Is the information reliable? Is it enough? We acquire a lot of information over the years—some more helpful than others. Advertisers will try to convince you that you need their products in order to be happy. Your friends may tell you that you need to have certain experiences to be happy—do drugs, smoke, drink, have sex. Others may tell you that you need money, fame or power to be happy. But what is God saying to you? That is the most vital information you need to know.

PSALM 27:11

Teach me your way, Lord;
lead me in a straight path

17. SAFETY

When I think of the first vehicles I drove, I shudder at how unsafe they were. They had no airbags to cushion a person in an accident. They had no seatbelts to keep people in the vehicle in the event of a rollover. They had no ABS breaking system to assist in slippery weather. The bumper was built like a battering ram with practically no energy-absorbing features. There were no headrests to reduce whiplash injuries, and there was no soft padding on the dashboard. Thankfully, today's vehicles have all these features and more to keep us much safer on the road.

Of course life has no guarantees. Even with all the safety improvements people still die in automobile accidents. But when it comes to our spiritual life, God has given us a guarantee. If we put our trust in Jesus we will get to Heaven. He has said that he has given us eternal life and no one is able to take that away from us. Apostle Paul testified that nothing in Heaven or Hell is able to separate us from the love of God, which is in Christ Jesus. It is like the old gospel song that says, "He will keep you from falling, he will keep to the end. What a wonderful Saviour, what a wonderful friend."

John 10:28

I give them eternal life, and they shall never perish; no one will snatch them out of my hand.

18. SECURITY

None of the vehicles I have ever owned have been on the "most stolen" list. Only someone desperate would steal a Vauxhall—although someone did steal the battery out of it. And then there was the K-car and an old Aerostar minivan, and a string of other practical but not-very-sought-after vehicles. Years ago it was fairly easy for thieves to "hot wire" cars. Even teens did this just to go on a joy ride, with no intentions of keeping the vehicles. Today security features are much improved with electronic keys, remote door locks and built-in GPS systems to track stolen cars.

In the Bible the devil is described as a thief who comes to take away that which God has given us. We see in the story of Adam and Eve how the devil stole their innocence and security. We see in the story of Noah how the devil took away peace from the earth and replaced it with violence. In the parable of the farmer scattering his seeds, the devil took away some of the word of the gospel before it could take root in the hearts of the hearers. We must be always on our guard against the devil, lest temptations of the world and the flesh rob us of our peace and the blessings we have in Jesus.

REVELATION 3:11

I am coming soon. Hold on to what you have, so that no one will take your crown.

19. ACCESSORIES

Car accessories are those things that make driving more pleasant. They are not necessities; you can drive without them, but they make the driving experience more enjoyable. My dad's old '54 pickup had one accessory—a glove compartment. By the time I got my '69 Vauxhall it had a glove compartment and a cigarette lighter (now called a power outlet). Later vehicles had a radio, cassette player, CD player and a satellite radio. Today's luxury vehicles have all this and more—heated seats, power seats, DVD player, heated steering wheel, climate control and built-in navigation system, to name a few.

In our Christian life there are also necessities and accessories. Certain things are absolutely necessary if we are to maintain a healthy spiritual lift— prayer, Bible reading, worship and fellowship with other Christians and acts of service. And there are other things that can help us, things that in this context may be considered accessories. These include listening to good music that will inspire us, reading good books that will encourage us and putting good art in our homes (including Christian art and mottos).

1 CORINTHIANS 10:31

So whether you eat or drink or whatever you do, do it all for the glory of God.

20. Mirrors

The rear-view mirrors are some of the most useful parts of your car. When I lend my car, people sometimes freak out by the way I have set my side mirrors, because when they look in them they cannot see what is behind them. I explain that the inside mirror is for seeing what is behind. The side mirrors are for covering blind spots. When a car is behind me it is in my inside mirror. When it disappears from that mirror it appears in one of my side mirrors. And when it disappears from those mirrors it appears in my peripheral eyesight. So I am always aware of exactly where other cars are at all times.

In life we should always be aware of where we are in relation to others and to where we have been. We go forward with our eyes on Jesus, but we must not turn a blind eye to those around us. We should be aware of those who are behind us. Some of them are following our example. Where we go, they will go. How we behave, they will behave. We should be aware of those coming alongside us in life. Some are there to encourage us. Some are there to reassure us. Some are there to help. And we should be aware of those overtaking us. Sooner or later we will slow down, our journey will end and others must complete the task and go where we cannot. We must be humble enough to let them pass.

2 Timothy 4:7

I have fought the good fight, I have finished the race, I have kept the faith.

Questions for Reflection and Discussion

1. What are some of the most exciting things about being a Christian?

2. What does it cost you to be a Christian?

3. How can a man filter out the bad or unnecessary things from his life?

4. How do you keep your cool under pressure?

5. How do you know when it's time to slow down?

6. What kind of maintenance schedule do you have for your faith?

7. What do you see when you look in the rear-view mirror of your life?

INSPIRATION IS ALL AROUND YOU

When Jesus taught, He used illustrations from everyday life. He spoke to people in language they could relate to: fishing (Matthew 4:18-19), building (Matthew 7:24-27), farming (Mark 4:1-20), baking (Matthew 13:33), weddings (Matthew 25:1-13), even washing dishes (Matthew 23:25-26).

Inspiration is all around us. We just have to take the time to reflect on life. A hymn-writer of long ago wrote:

"God speaks to us in bird and song,
In winds that drift the clouds along"

(Joseph Johnson, 1848-1926)

Another wrote:

"In the rustling grass I hear him pass,
He speaks to me everywhere."

(Maltbie Davenport Babcock, 1858-1901)

Most of us find inspiration at church as we listen to a sermon or the choir, share in corporate prayer, or sing along with others in the congregation. But God speaks through the everyday events of our lives as well—while we are driving, involved in sports, working or engaged in some hobby. We just have to listen.

Jesus said, "I am with you always." He's not just there at church. He is also with us in the boat, on the golf course, on the assembly line, on the sidewalk. He speaks to us everywhere.

As you live your life, take time every day to be inspired.

CPSIA information can be obtained
at www.ICGtesting.com
Printed in the USA
LVHW092050081119
636839LV00001B/5/P

9 781400 325368